3/92

n
ya

D102240G

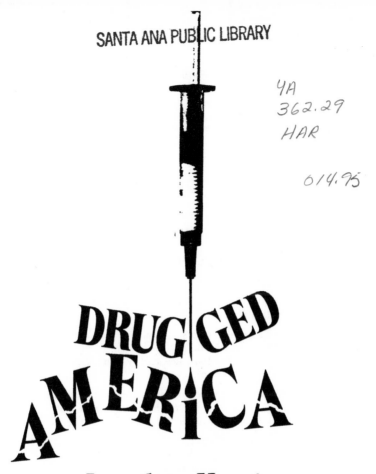

DRUGGED AMERICA

Jonathan Harris

FOUR WINDS PRESS
New York

COLLIER MACMILLAN CANADA
Toronto

MAXWELL MACMILLAN INTERNATIONAL PUBLISHING GROUP
New York · Oxford · Singapore · Sydney

Four Winds Press
Macmillan Publishing Company
866 Third Avenue
New York, NY 10022
Collier Macmillan Canada, Inc.
1200 Eglinton Avenue East
Suite 200
Don Mills, Ontario M3C 3N1
First edition
Printed and bound in the United States of America

10 9 8 7 6 5 4 3 2 1

The text of this book is set in 12 point Century Old Style.
Designed by REM Studio, Inc.

The quote that appears on page 87 is from *The Pharmacist's Guide
to the Most Misused and Abused Drugs in America* by Ken Liska.
Copyright © 1988 by Ken Liska. Reprinted by permission of
Macmillan Publishing Company.

Grateful acknowledgment is made to James A. Inciardi for permission
to quote from *The War on Drugs: Heroin, Cocaine, Crime, and
Public Policy* (Mountain View, Calif.: Mayfield, 1984) on page 113.

Special thanks to Peter F. Pinto, Ph.D., clinical director of
Samaritan Village, Inc., for checking the facts in this book and
providing valuable statistical information; and to Jack Gustafson,
deputy director, New York State Division of Substance Abuse Services,
for his help in putting us in touch with Dr. Pinto.

Harris, Jonathan.
        Drugged America / Jonathan Harris. — 1st ed.
                p.   cm.
        Includes bibliographical references and index.
        Summary: Examines the drug crisis in America, discussing the
politics of drug warfare, current measures being taken against
narcotics addiction and trade, and realistic goals for the future
of the "war on drugs."
        ISBN 0-02-742745-5
        1. Drug abuse—United States—Juvenile literature. 2. Narcotics,
Control of—United States—Juvenile literature. 3. Drug traffic—
United States—Juvenile literature. [1. Drug abuse.
2. Narcotics, Control of. 3. Drug traffic.] I. Title.
HV5825.H273 1991
362.29′0973—dc20   90-47649

WHAT ARE THE MOST HARMFUL EFFECTS OF DRUGS?

Drugs
are used
to prevent the
Pain
in every heart. For
every teardrop that falls, another
pill is popped.
Yet the
Pain returns;
family,
friends,
all feel the
emptiness, the
silence. The
hurt, the
anger,
all return.
The user
loses reality, and
so the
Pain returns.
The
Pain
. . . Returns.

(Written by an anonymous youngster for an antidrug writing contest sponsored by a Long Island newspaper, Fall 1989)

Contents

1

Snapshots from Drugged America

Senseless violence. Self-destructive addiction. Wrenching grief. Pervading fear. Soul-destroying greed. Corruption in high places. Tragicomic bumbling. Redeeming courage and kindness. Shining compassion. Hard-won recovery. These are random impressions of America in the throes of the drug epidemic. Here are some specific ones—snapshots from the 1980s and early 1990s.

• • •

In March 1983, Rosa Montoya de Hernandez arrived in Los Angeles by plane from Bogotá, Colombia. She fit the U.S. Customs Service's profile of an "alimentary smuggler," a person who smuggles drugs by concealing them inside his or her own digestive (alimentary) system. Mrs. Montoya was

1

held for over twenty-four hours, strip-searched, and ordered to have a bowel movement. She resisted as long as she could but finally excreted a balloon filled with cocaine. Over the next four days, she excreted no fewer than 88 additional balloons, weighing a total of 1.2 pounds.

Montoya was tried and convicted. She appealed on the ground that she had been subjected to an "unreasonable search," a violation of the Fourth Amendment to the Constitution. The U.S. Supreme Court upheld her conviction. The Court ruled that the Customs officers had a right to conduct this "search" because their information about her justified their suspicion.

• • •

A former addict was exulting in the San Francisco office of drug therapist Joanne Baum. He had been clean for two months, after using drugs for twenty years, starting at age fifteen. He was now experiencing and appreciating life as he never had while under the influence. But, as Baum wrote in a 1985 book, she felt it necessary to warn him: "You're not going to feel this good, this high, all the time; it is unrealistic. . . . Feelings come in waves, the good waves come and go, the bad waves come and go. . . . Wanting to feel good all the time is addictive thinking."

• • •

Until 1987, the children of Roosevelt, New York, had to find someplace to play other than their town's Centennial Park. Drug dealers had taken it over.

Then three hundred members of the almost entirely black community marched into the park and ordered the dealers out. Most prominent among the determined townspeople were Muslims from the Ta-Ha Mosque, which operates a school. The Muslims now patrol the area periodically, shadow any dealers they find, and report them to the police.

"When the Muslims walk through," said park director Willie White, "those who are doing wrong stop and move on out of respect."

Inspector Robert McGuigan, deputy commander of the local precinct, is delighted. "The community spirit has been terrific. As long as we are both going in the same direction and not acting like vigilantes, we can have an even greater impact."

• • •

It may have been one of the most ingenious smuggling techniques ever invented. It involved a shipment of tropical fish addressed to a San Francisco importer in March 1988. Two million dollars worth of heroin had been packaged in small amounts, wrapped in cellophane, and inserted into the bodies of live goldfish. The shipment traveled on a complex route. The heroin had originated in the Golden Triangle opium-growing area on the remote borders of Laos, Thailand, and Myanmar (formerly Burma). Chinese drug agents intercepted it in Shanghai.

• • •

On a fall day in 1988, Detective Pat DeGregorio noticed a group of teenagers gathered around a van parked in a lane in Kings Park, Long Island, New York. He turned his car back for a second look. All but one of the youngsters scattered. A tall, blond girl just stood there, a paper bag at her feet. It turned out to contain marijuana, cocaine, and LSD. DeGregorio was devastated to recognize his own sixteen-year-old daughter, Mary Anne.

The stunned detective couldn't bring himself to arrest

Mary Anne. He took her home and flushed the drugs down the toilet. He couldn't understand how he and his wife, Barbara—also a narcotics detective—could have been so blind for so long.

Only now, in the course of a long and stormy talk with Mary Anne, did they learn that the girl had started drinking secretly at twelve. First she tried beer, then whiskey. Then she tried drugs. By the time she was fifteen, Mary Anne was psychologically addicted to marijuana, amphetamines, cocaine, and LSD.

The next step was inevitable. Needing money for the drugs, she started dealing. To hide what she was doing, she used every trick she'd learned by observing her parents' professional police techniques over the years.

But now, to her outraged parents, she denied that she had a drug habit and brazenly defied them. They threw her out of the house. She could return only when she agreed to seek help.

Weeks later, DeGregorio found Mary Anne dead drunk and unconscious, under the bar in the basement. She had sneaked in the night before. Later, they talked. "I want help," Mary Anne confessed.

The DeGregorios placed her in a residential treatment center. Nearly a year later, she was still there, hoping another six months might make a difference. She had earned her high-school diploma, but cravings for the narcotics that had wrecked her life still bedeviled her.

Mary Anne may go into the field of fashion design someday. Or perhaps, like some recovering addicts on the treatment center's staff, she will become a drug counselor.

• • •

Los Alamos National Laboratory in New Mexico is a top-secret center for research on nuclear weapons. A Los Alamos computer technician with high-level security clearance was arrested in October 1988 with two hundred pounds of marijuana in his truck. A congressional committee began an investigation into reports of drug use at the laboratory.

This was not the first such investigation. The U.S. government's watchdog agency, the General Accounting Office, was already looking into possible drug use at the Lawrence Livermore National Laboratory in California. It, too, is a nuclear-weapons research plant. Some scientific equipment and a number of classified documents had disappeared. A 1986 undercover operation had already turned up the names of 127 suspected drug users and dealers at the lab. Six employees were arrested and ten others forced to resign. But the laboratory's managers halted the inquiry before it was extended into the most highly classified areas.

No one knew how deeply or dangerously the drug epidemic had infected these extremely sensitive security installations. Congressional probers were trying to penetrate the mystery, but months of investigation lay ahead.

• • •

For New York City, 1988 was the bloodiest year ever. The year's 1,842d homicide, just after Christmas, broke a seven-year record. "There's no question that the sharply mounting incidence of murders is directly tied to the increased use of drugs," said the Queens district attorney, John J. Santucci. About half the slayings were said to be linked in some way to drugs. Among the victims were children living in areas of contested drug turf, bystanders caught in the cross-fire on the streets, members of drug gangs, robbery victims killed by addicts, and police officers killed in the line of duty.

• • •

Directors of shelters for battered women are concerned about a disturbing new trend. Not only are the number of calls from abused women increasing, but more women than ever are calling because of their abusers' drug problems. Cocaine and crack, they report, seem to turn their live-in companions and husbands toward violence much more than marijuana, heroin, or alcohol have ever done.

• • •

In Wyandanch, New York, a ten-year-old boy was arrested for selling crack. He may be the youngest drug dealer ever picked up by police. He was working with a fourteen-year-old partner.

It is not unusual for children to "hold" drugs for adult dealers, so that the adults will have nothing on them if arrested. Kids who do this are known as "layaways." But this youngster was not just holding. The police observed him exchanging drugs for money six times. When the boy realized the cops were watching him, he pulled a brown paper bag from his pocket and dropped it to the ground. It contained three "jumbos"—large rocks of crack worth twenty dollars each. The cops say he had $154 in cash in his pocket.

A family court judge sentenced the boy to eighteen months in a home for troubled children.

He is part of a new and rapidly growing child labor force. Its young members claim to make from two hundred to two thousand dollars a week from the crack trade. In 1988, more than 130 youngsters under the age of sixteen were arrested on drug charges on Long Island, New York, alone. Thousands of other juveniles were being held in jails across the country.

● ● ●

In West Perrine, Florida, a community near Miami, grocery-store owner Lee Arthur Lawrence had been waging a lonely war against the drug dealers for years. He chased them out of his store's parking lot, worked with the police to sweep the dealers from the streets, and visited schools to preach the dangers of drug and alcohol abuse. His war became so well known that the *Miami Herald* published a feature about him in March 1987.

Dealers tried to kill Lawrence three times after the article appeared. He had taken to carrying a gun. Once when he was shot at, he returned fire but missed. He repeatedly asked for special police protection, but the police replied that many people received threats on their lives and the police were not equipped to provide "security around the clock."

On March 23, 1989, Lee Lawrence's courageous war ended. Standing in the doorway of his store, he was caught in a hail of bullets. The police believe two hired professional killers carried out the hit. Nobody has been arrested as yet.

● ● ●

"Everybody is making money selling drugs. It's pretty swift money." The speaker was a nineteen-year-old crack dealer who said his name was Ham. He was standing on a street corner in Washington, D.C., just a few minutes' ride from the White House. He had a wad of ten- and twenty-dollar bills in his pocket.

Ham was conscious of the risks. "Right off, I can think of four people I know who got killed. A dude named Lonnie got shot right over there. He owed somebody money. You don't pay your debts, you get shot. It's the principle."

The regional chairman of the District of Columbia United Way, Jeffery M. Johnson, interviewed dozens of drug dealers in prison and on the streets. In March 1989, he described many of them as "street yuppies." To them, drugs are "a vehicle to obtain whatever America has to offer. They are completely ruthless about protecting what they have. The only thing they connect to is the money aspect of life."

• • •

In Detroit, a Little League team broke up in the spring of 1989. Its members were making too much money selling crack to play baseball.

• • •

Also in Detroit, a car pulled up near a house at about two o'clock in the morning. A woman got out and walked down the driveway alongside the house. From a window on the second floor, a drug dealer lowered a cup. She put the required amount of money in it. When it came back down to her, it held a little plastic bag of crack. She got back in her car and drove away, but another car pulled up almost immediately. Within fifteen minutes, twenty sales were made and at least two hundred dollars changed hands.

The dealers at this house had been selling from the ground floor, but the police had broken all the windows at that level. The new method seemed safer.

• • •

Still in Detroit, crack dealers took over an abandoned house on a working-class street. The neighborhood changed, according to the *New York Times,* "to a place where bands of teenagers shot at each other in daylight, sold drugs from the curb, and sneered at people who threatened to call the police." Two fed-up residents burned the crack house down. At their trial, they defiantly admitted it. The jury acquitted them.

• • •

In Brownsville, Texas, twelve members of a Mexican drug-smuggling ring kidnaped a twenty-one-year-old University of Texas medical student named Mark Kilroy. They took him to the Santa Elena cattle and sorghum ranch near Matamoros, just across the border in Mexico. There they murdered him as part of a bizarre ritual that they believed would make them immune to arrest and prosecution. They belonged to a Satan-worshiping cult responsible for shipping a ton of marijuana into the U.S. every month.

When Mexican police explored the murder site in April 1989, they unearthed the remains of at least thirteen other individuals, some of them badly mutilated and dismembered. Captured members of the cult said that their *padrino* (god-father), or leader—twenty-six-year-old Adolfo de Jesus Constanzo, a Cuban from Miami—had done the actual killings. Constanzo subsequently died during a shootout with police. Preferring death to arrest, he ordered one of the gang members to shoot him.

Constanzo's closest companion, twenty-four-year-old Sara Maria Villareal Aldrete, was arrested after the shootout. She had been living a double life. At Texas Southmost College in Brownsville, she was known as a model student and president of the booster club. But in her apartment south of the border, police found a bloody candle-strewn altar, along with blood-spattered children's clothes and stained walls. Mexican

police believed her to be the cult's "priestess" and took to
calling her a witch.

• • •

In the drug-ridden Liberty City district of Miami, Carrie
Edmundson was sitting at her picnic table on a steamy day.
She had tried to make her home an oasis for the local kids.
Seventeen of them were playing in her front yard.

A scuffle broke out among the youthful drug pushers
who had taken over the neighborhood. One badly beaten
youth sought refuge in Edmundson's house. Her adult son
let him in. The other dealers left, but one of them soon
returned, seeking revenge. Standing outside the gate that
was meant to protect the children, he opened fire with a
.357 Magnum.

Edmundson's son was hit in the leg and buttocks. Eight-
year-old Chelsea Wiley died instantly, cut down while playing
ring-around-a-rosy. Edmundson's granddaughter, Jennifer
Royal, was hit in the back just a quarter-inch from her spinal
cord. Two slugs slammed into three-year-old Adrian
Robinson's wrist and shoulder.

Police arrived and arrested the gunman. One officer wept.

• • •

In San Francisco, Louise Vaughn was raising two of her
grandchildren, one five years old and the other two. "It's not
a fond thing, a joy thing," she said. "Starting all over again,
with the PTA, Girl Scouts—I don't look forward to that."

Louise Vaughn is not exceptional. An astonishing number of grandmothers, many worn out by age, poverty, and
sorrow, have been forced into parenting all over again. The
children's own parents are lost to crack.

• • •

Health authorities on Long Island became alarmed in the spring of 1989 about a steep rise in the incidence of sexually transmitted diseases. These had spread almost in direct proportion to the spread of crack. Dennis Murphy, director of New York State's program for treating these infections, said the problems on Long Island reflected a nationwide trend that began in the cities. "There is no question that crack use and sexually transmitted diseases go hand in hand," he said.

Murphy added that 70 to 80 percent of the syphilis cases in Suffolk County were directly related to the use of crack. The drug is thought to stimulate pathological levels of sexual activity. Prostitutes addicted to it are a particular source of danger. To get money to buy crack, Murphy asserted, "they may have fifteen partners a day."

Health experts throughout the nation have noted another alarming result of the spread of syphilis and other venereal diseases that cause breaks in the skin. The new epidemic has brought along with it a rise in the incidence of Acquired Immune Deficiency Syndrome (AIDS) stemming from heterosexual contact. There is no known cure for AIDS, an infectious disease that takes over the body's immune system. The skin lesions caused by venereal diseases provide easy doorways for the AIDS virus to be transmitted between men and women.

• • •

Police staged what was probably the biggest drug raid in the history of Washington, D.C., in mid-April 1989. They arrested eighteen people. Police officials boasted at first that they had eliminated one of the largest and most violent cocaine-distribution operations in the District of Columbia. Within two weeks, however, they had to admit that other drug dealers had already moved in to fill the gap. Cocaine and crack were as plentiful as ever on the streets of the capital. The raid had no effect on the drugs' street price.

The Washington murder rate, highest in the nation, continued at such a pace that year that the city was dubbed the "murder capital of the world." Most of this was due to drug-related violence. Over three hundred drug dealers and users had been killed there over the past several years. The rate rose rapidly. When 369 drug-linked killings were reported between January 1 and November 1, 1989, the murder rate already equaled the total for the entire previous year. A record 438 people were slain in drug-related homicides in all of 1989. And during the first 11 months of 1990, a total of 436 people were slain despite a slight decline in drug abuse.

• • •

In Winnebago County, Illinois, state attorney Paul Logli charged twenty-four-year-old Melanie Green with involuntary manslaughter. Her two-day-old baby girl had died. Green had allegedly been taking cocaine during her pregnancy, and the baby was born addicted. She weighed a mere 4 pounds 3 ounces, well below normal birth weight. Tests suggested the drug had caused irreparable damage to her heart and brain. Traveling through the placenta, which links the mother's body to the baby's, the drug had apparently prevented the embryo from getting the oxygen it needed.

The charge is believed to be the most serious ever made in the U.S. against a mother whose drug use was alleged to have harmed her baby.

Health and social-service professionals disapproved of

the criminal charge. They argued it was an ineffective scare tactic that would only frighten drug-abusing women from seeking help that is already too scarce. Logli contended that the prosecution was necessary to "fix responsibility to deter others from committing the same acts."

The grand jury turned down Logli's arguments and refused to indict Melanie Green.

•   •   •

In Tampa, Florida, eleven men were arrested when they came to what they thought was going to be a bachelor party preceding the wedding of two friends. They had received engraved wedding invitations: "We invite you to be with us as we begin our new life together."

The friends turned out to be members of a team of undercover drug agents. The agents had spent two years investigating a complex scheme that involved the "laundering" of millions of dollars in drug money. The eleven "guests" had already been indicted for their parts in the laundering transactions.

•   •   •

In San Francisco, clients were coming to the Stimulant Abuse Recovery Center for their daily acupuncture treatment. One of them, Leon Franklin, told a *Newsweek* interviewer that he was thirteen when he started on dope. "I've used everything, but I ended up on crack and booze. You need the booze to calm you when you're wrecked on crack."

At this clinic, the acupuncture procedure was done by the painless placing of needles in addicts' ears. No one knew why it seemed to ease the symptoms of drug withdrawal. The center's director, Tony Landrum, claimed an 80 percent success rate. He had used the needles, along with counseling, vitamins, and herbal tea, on more than five hundred crack addicts at a previous clinic.

Landrum claimed success whenever random urine testing at the end of the treatment period showed that the addicts were no longer using crack. But he'd never had the funds for the more extensive study that might have shown how many remained clean for weeks, months, or years afterward.

• • •

In the escalating war between Los Angeles's dominant gangs, the Crips and the Bloods, a favorite expression for killing someone is "boo-yah," imitating the sound of a sawed-off shotgun. "We average a murder a day in South Central," Deputy Chief William Rathburn of the L.A. Police Department told *U. S. News & World Report* in 1989. "We have drive-by shootings with great regularity." He blamed "the competition for drug sales" for the increase in gang violence. The stacks of money the gangs were taking in were providing them with sophisticated weapons: "They buy the AK-47 and a case of ammunition."

Residents in the most fought-over areas do not use their front rooms at night for fear of indiscriminate shootings. Many will not turn on the lights at night. Some have told Rathburn they sleep on the floor to avoid random shots from drive-bys.

• • •

On January 19, 1990, the citizens of Washington, D.C., were stunned to learn that their mayor, Marion Barry, had been arrested the night before on charges of drug possession and perjury. A lady friend, who also happened to be one of the country's top models, had lured him to a downtown hotel room. There he had allegedly been observed—and video-taped—smoking crack.

It was all part of an undercover "sting" operation set up by the FBI and the Washington police. The lady was operating under their direction.

This was not the first time that Barry had been accused of drug involvement. Law-enforcement authorities had had the mayor under surveillance for many weeks. Despite the strong evidence against him, he denied using drugs. Soon after his arraignment, Barry left Washington to enter a treatment center in Florida. He insisted that he needed treatment only for alcoholism. Close associates told reporters that Barry did have a drug problem.

The day after his arrest, Mayor Barry had been expected to announce that he would run for a fourth term. Instead, he faced ten charges of drug possession, one charge of conspiracy to obtain and use drugs, and three charges of lying to a grand jury. His ten-week trial ended in August 1990, with the jury convicting him on only one misdemeanor drug-possession charge, acquitting him of another, and reporting itself unable to reach a verdict on the remaining charges.

In September 1990, the prosecutor announced that he would not retry Barry on the remaining charges. A month later, Barry was sentenced to six months in prison, a $5,000 fine, continued drug treatment, regular testing for drugs, and one year's probation following his release. His attorney pledged to appeal the sentence.

• • •

Stories like these raise many questions. Where do the drugs come from? How do they get here? What can be done—and what is being done—to stop them?

2

Cocaine International

Three drugs dominate the American scene today: cocaine, heroin, and marijuana. Cocaine, or "coke," is the fastest rising in popularity. In its powdered form, it is most commonly enjoyed by "snorting," or inhaling through one nostril at a time. In the form of crack, it is smoked through a glass pipe.

Heroin abuse seems to have leveled off. The use of marijuana has probably declined slightly in recent years, though pot smokers still outnumber all other drug users. Hashish, a somewhat stronger stimulant, is derived from the same plant as marijuana but is less widely used.

There are, of course, numerous other drugs on the market. They include the various types of sedatives and tranquilizers ("downers"), such as Valium and codeine. Opposite in effect are the stimulants ("uppers"), such as amphetamines and methamphetamine ("speed"). The newest innovation is a smokeable form of methamphetamine ("ice").

Some experts predict that ice will become the popular drug of the 1990s, even replacing crack. Ice gives a much longer high than crack does, in some cases lasting twenty-four hours. But ice's extraordinary high is followed by a "crash" or depression so profound that it resembles a severe mental disease, paranoid schizophrenia.

Some users who regard themselves as connoisseurs prefer the synthetic narcotics ("designer drugs"). Individuals hoping to build their muscle mass go for the anabolic steroids. Hallucinogens such as LSD and PCP ("angel dust") are available for those seeking mind-blowing "trips." Each type of drug has its own following, but compared to the big three the sales of these more specialized drugs are relatively small.

Until recently, cocaine, heroin, and marijuana were produced mainly abroad. This is still true of cocaine and heroin, but an increasing share of the marijuana smoked by Americans is grown here, in this country.

THE LORDS OF COCAINE

In the early 1970s, the cocaine racket in the U.S. was controlled by Cubans in Miami. They sold it mostly to fellow Cubans. Then demand began to rise among the American public, which meant new opportunities for profit for the drug sellers.

That brought in the Colombians. They had already won access to the big East Coast markets through their well-established marijuana networks. War broke out between the Colombian and the Cuban drug dealers. The nation was stunned as it witnessed high-speed machine-gun battles on the roads. One bloody battle took place in a south Florida shopping mall.

The Colombians soon took over most of the market.

Powdered cocaine was relatively expensive. That made it a luxury, affordable mostly by the well-to-do. It was highly profitable for the drug kingpins, but they were unsatisfied. They were eager to penetrate the larger mass market, where the profits would be astronomical.

Crack was the solution to the problem. Introduced in the early 1980s, this is a highly addictive form of cocaine in the shape of little "rocks." It was selling in the late 1980s for as little as ten dollars a dose, but it has since become even cheaper. Crack supposedly got its name from the crackling sound it makes when smoked.

It gives an extremely intense, irresistibly pleasurable high. Unfortunately for the user—but fortunately for the drug dealer—the crack high lasts only a few minutes. The user craves another smoke almost at once—and then another, and then another. Addiction develops faster than with any other drug. Crack addicts quickly discover that they have to spend more money on their "cheap" habit than they ever needed for any other kind of high.

Crack is made by mixing cocaine powder with baking soda and water, then subjecting the mixture to certain treatments. The whole process can be accomplished quickly and inexpensively in about twenty minutes.

THE COLOMBIAN CARTELS

Profiting most from the American crack fad today is a small group of South American cocaine producers, processors, and exporters. The richest and most powerful of them are the Colombians. Their country is a small one on the northern coast of South America.

These Colombian drug lords have their main headquarters in Medellín, the country's second-largest city. They operate in a loosely organized group known as the "Medellín cartel." A second, much smaller, cartel operates out of the town of Cali.

The biggest difference between them is that the Medellín cartel relies heavily on violence and terror. It actively supports extreme right-wing politicians and seems intent on seizing control of the Colombian government.

The Cali group prefers bribery to gunplay. It stays aloof from politics and avoids confrontation with the government. It is also believed to run a more efficient and businesslike organization than do the Medellín mobsters, and probably ships more cocaine to the U.S. every year.

Through the 1970s and early 1980s, these cartels went unrecognized by antidrug authorities. It was assumed that hundreds of small traffickers controlled the flow of drugs. Then, in March 1982, agents of the U.S. Drug Enforcement Administration discovered nearly two tons of pure cocaine concealed in a cargo of blue jeans imported to Florida from Colombia. So large a shipment could only have been planned and carried out by a large, well-coordinated organization. Further investigation turned up the two cartels.

Like the owner-managers of other big businesses, the

cocaine kingpins keep a tight control over their product at every stage. First they purchase the coca leaves from the peasants of Peru, Bolivia, and other neighboring countries in the Andean region of northwest South America. These peasants have been accustomed for centuries to chewing the coca leaf for its mild stimulating qualities. The coca leaf contains only about .5 to 1 percent cocaine.

The Andean peoples also use the leaf to make tea. Coca tea is routinely sold in the form of commercial tea bags in hotels and restaurants throughout the area.

Cocaine cultivation has increased so rapidly in recent years that the market is glutted. The Colombian government's recently launched crackdown on major drug traffickers, and Bolivia's stepped-up assaults on drug laboratories and major buyers of coca paste, have also slowed the demand for coca leaves. They once sold for as much as $400 to $500 for 100 pounds. Today 100 pounds of coca leaves can be purchased in Bolivia for as little as $5 to $7. Some Bolivian farmers are switching to other crops.

Some of the more enterprising peasants carry out the first step in the processing of the coca leaf. They transform the leaves into the more valuable coca paste and sell that to the big dealers. Five 50-pound bags of coca leaf make one kilo of coca paste. (One kilogram, or kilo, equals 2.2 pounds.) The paste is usually about 40 percent pure cocaine, though it can be up to 90 percent pure.

For the peasants, these products make the difference between poverty and a decent standard of living. The coca bush yields three harvests a year and lives for fifteen to thirty years. One hectare (2.471 acres) can produce about 2,000 kilos (4,400 pounds) of leaves per year. Where the average peasant earns a wretched $160 a year, coca producers can take in as much as $1,000. That amounts to a veritable fortune for these impoverished folk.

An estimated 1.5 million people are employed in cocaine production throughout the Andean region. They inevitably resist U.S. efforts to get these countries' governments to reduce coca cultivation or to substitute other crops. More coca was planted in 1989 than was replaced. The three Andean countries of Colombia, Peru, and Bolivia supply the world market with an annual total of at least 400 metric tons of cocaine.

Coca leaf and paste form important export items in the economies of Peru and Bolivia. Peru reaps up to $1.5 billion a year from coca sales. Oil, once the country's biggest money-maker, has gone down in price, making coca comparatively more profitable.

In Bolivia, the export of legal goods earns about $800 million a year. The income from cocaine probably exceeds that amount. The flood of drug earnings for years enabled the drug lords to bribe officials at all levels, both in the government and in the army.

In 1980 the drug traffickers actually won absolute control of the Bolivian government. They paid General Luis Garcia Meza over $1 million to stage a coup and take over the government. Once in power, Meza conducted a reign of terror, during which many honest officials were killed and drug-crime records destroyed. Fortunately, a legitimate government came into office in 1982. It has striven to cooperate with American antidrug programs ever since.

In 1986, Bolivia invited the U.S. to dispatch a helicopter-borne military force, along with Drug Enforcement Administration (DEA) agents, to help with the largest raid ever carried out against the drug laboratories in the jungles. These laboratories refine the coca paste into cocaine powder. The raid was so successful that it temporarily shut down all coke refining in Bolivia. The labs have since resumed operations in new locations, however.

This was not the first major raid by the Bolivian authorities. In 1984 they discovered a massive complex of air-conditioned laboratories in a jungle location called Tranquilandia. They quickly found five more complexes within seventy-five miles. By the time the raid was completed, the police had taken possession of seven aircraft, forty-four buildings, six airstrips, nine laboratories, a world's record ten tons of cocaine and cocaine base, 10,000 fifty-five-gallon drums of ether, and other chemicals used in processing the drugs.

Even this massive blow did not result in a scarcity of cocaine. Its price had been expected to rise steeply because the huge seizures by the police were predicted to produce a shortage in the marketplace. Instead, the price remained steady. There were ample other sources available.

The U.S. has also carried out joint raids with the Peruvians. In September 1989, helicopter raids employing teams of Peruvian police and American DEA agents uncovered and destroyed a number of labs in the Upper Huallaga Valley. This is the center of coca-leaf cultivation, where about two-thirds of the world's coca crop is grown. Some 300,000 Peruvian farmers are involved in coca farming.

Since that first raid, the Peruvian-American teams have destroyed nineteen labs and twelve airfields. But officials admit that these efforts have so far had little effect on the enormous Peruvian coca industry. The crop has been expanding by about 10 percent a year and is thought to have grown by 20 percent in 1989.

The U.S. has supplied millions of dollars to promote these countries' agriculture. American officials feel strongly that coca cultivation prevents the development of an agriculture that would feed the people and provide the raw materials for a wholesome trade with other countries.

Some experts believe there is only one way the Andean peasants will ever be persuaded to replace the profitable coca with other crops. The U.S. would have to subsidize them (pay them to make the change). But such a program would be extremely expensive. The U.S. has already promised $2.2 billion in military, economic, and law-enforcement aid to the three countries over the five years starting in 1990. Even that sizable amount will scarcely begin to compensate for what these people stand to lose.

American antidrug efforts in these countries have also run into a contradictory American determination not to do anything that might weaken or destabilize their governments. Two American campaigns collide head-on in this part of the world: the drive against drugs and the drive against radical revolutionaries.

Some influential American foreign-policy officials feel that strengthening the Andean countries' resistance to left-wing subversion is more important than reducing their drug production. They theorize that elimination of drug revenues would further impoverish the already suffering peasants and could well lead to political turmoil that would favor a radical left-wing takeover.

In Peru, a radical leftist guerrilla movement known as the *Sendero Luminoso* ("Shining Path") has disrupted U.S.-backed antidrug campaigns as part of its drive against "American imperialism." By January 1989, the guerrilla attacks had become so troublesome that some forty American antidrug agents had to give up their operations and leave their head-quarters town, Tingo Maria.

Peru's Upper Huallaga valley stretches 200 miles north of Tingo Maria. Some 250,000 acres are under cultivation, supplying the raw material for half the cocaine consumed in the U.S.

The Shining Path revolutionaries are known to be strongly opposed to drug use, but they recognize how important the income from coca is to the peasants. They launch powerful guerrilla attacks on the government forces sent to eradicate the coca crops, and they even intervene to make sure the peasants get a good price from the processors.

In April 1990, the U.S. and Peru agreed to send American military trainers to Peru to help fight the Shining Path guerrillas. A new training base has been built in the heart of the coca-growing area. The trainers are members of the Green Berets. They are under orders to stay inside the base and avoid taking part in any operations. In addition, Peru received a $35 million military-aid package.

Even when they are not being stirred up by revolutionary guerrillas, peasants' resentment of antidrug agents in all three countries has sometimes erupted into violence. When a team of Colombian agents seized sixty kilos of coca paste in Bolivia's Chapare province, a mob of two hundred peasants tortured, mutilated, and murdered them. In Peru, peasants attacked a camp manned by seventeen members of the Peruvian civil guard and killed them all.

Vast areas of the Peruvian and Bolivian jungles are being burned off so that settlers can grow more coca. In the Beni area in Bolivia's northern region and in the centrally located Chapare rain forest near the city of Cochabamba, production keeps rising. Only in the Yungas region, around the capital city of La Paz, have government forces, encouraged by the U.S., destroyed significant portions of the local coca economy.

Wherever the plant is under active cultivation, ugly red gashes can be seen in the jungle clay. These are landing strips for planes that fly the coca paste to laboratories hidden in the jungles. Though most of the labs are located in Colombia, many have been hidden throughout the coca-producing areas of Peru and Bolivia as well.

The CIA and other federal agencies recently began using space satellites to spy out the maze of secret airstrips, roads, laboratories, and escape routes used by the smugglers throughout the Andean region. The satellites are also useful for spotting remote areas where coca is grown. They have been giving special attention to the Upper Huallaga valley, which is dotted with labs, hideouts, and about sixty airstrips.

The optical and photo equipment carried by the satellites is so accurate that it can read a license plate from hundreds of miles in space. Eventually the satellites will take on the tough job of tracking drug-carrying ships and planes.

When the processors have refined the raw materials into a highly purified form of cocaine powder, they arrange its shipment to the United States. In some cases they even oversee its distribution within the American market.

This last stage is the most profitable of all. The South American cocaine trade is estimated to bring in over $4 billion per year. Of this, the Colombians take about $3 billion.

Such huge amounts of readily available cash can have upsetting effects on world markets. In Miami, for example, some of these "cocaine cowboys" have been known to walk into real-estate offices with suitcases full of currency. They would buy a luxurious canal-front villa for $1 million and pay cash for it on the spot. Houses that had been selling for $300,000 a year earlier are suddenly bringing in three and four times as much.

SHIPPING THE COKE

The drug traffickers face a vigorous U.S. effort to track the drug shipments and seize them either before they reach the American border or as soon as they arrive. The cartels have had to develop extensive networks of alternate routes and means of transport. For years, the primary area of entry into the U.S. was southern Florida, with New York the second choice. The drug was usually shipped in lots of several hundred kilos.

Because of the distance from Colombia to Florida (1,100 miles to Miami), the small planes that carry the drugs have to either refuel somewhere along the way or transship their drug loads to other planes. The smugglers often arrange this by bribing government officials in various Caribbean countries, notably the Bahamas and formerly in Panama. The newest wrinkle is long-range planes, capable of flying from Colombia to the Caribbean area, dumping their loads, and then flying back without stopping to be refueled.

For some years Cuba was another favorite stopover point. But in June 1989, a military honor tribunal convicted one of the country's most-decorated officers, General Arnaldo Ochoa. He was found guilty of conspiring with the Medellín cartel to smuggle cocaine through Cuba to the U.S.

Ochoa was stripped of his medals, expelled from the army, found guilty of high treason against the fatherland, and summarily executed. The harsh treatment he got probably meant the end of Cuba's role in the international drug trade—at least for the time being.

But the bosses of the Medellín cartel have not always had to rely on buying the goodwill of foreign officials. One of the cocaine kingpins, Carlos Lehder Rivas, owned his own private island, called Norman's Cay, in the Bahamas. He built a 3,000-foot runway there to accommodate the cartel's drug-laden planes. The traffic went on day and night, making millions for him.

Lehder was the most flamboyant member of the Medellín command. He had founded his own extreme right-wing party in Colombia. Its rallies seemed impressive, drawing big crowds. But an enterprising reporter discovered that Lehder paid each member of the audience 1,000 pesos (about 35 cents) to attend, a great deal of money to these poor peasants. He was fascinated by Adolf Hitler, whom he deemed "the greatest warrior in history."

During a visit to Colombia in 1989, Lehder was spotted by the police and arrested. The authorities knew there was little chance of a successful prosecution in Colombia. Lehder could call in his private army of machine-gun–wielding gangsters to ensure his escape. He could bribe or intimidate any prosecutor or judge who dared to try his case.

Colombia had, however, signed an extradition treaty with the U.S. in 1982. *Extradition* means that a criminal arrested in one country can be sent to another country in which he has been charged with a crime. Lehder had been indicted for drug trafficking by two grand juries in Florida. He became the first Medellín kingpin extradited to the U.S. There he was swiftly tried, convicted, and sentenced to life imprisonment.

Drug smugglers who use planes to carry drugs into the

U.S. often have the pilots dump their cargoes into the water at certain designated spots. The plane can then land at any U.S. airport and pass successfully through a customs inspection. Meanwhile fast speedboats race out to the exact spot pinpointed by radio, find the drugs, and haul them aboard. Those on the boat can easily pretend to be honest fishermen, knowing that small boats based in U.S. ports do not normally have to undergo inspection when they return to port.

Another favorite method is to ship large quantities of drugs on big "mother ships." These anchor well off the twelve-mile limit. This places them in international waters, where the U.S. Coast Guard cannot legally interfere with them. Specially built "cigarette boats," so fast that the Coast Guard cannot overtake them, hustle the drug cargoes to shore in the dead of night.

But the largest quantities of drugs, amounting to perhaps half of all the narcotics entering the U.S., arrive sealed into the huge steel containers that are today's most common method of shipping goods in bulk. They flood directly into New York and other East Coast port cities. As law-enforcement officials block other drug routes more and more effectively, the oceangoing container ships are increasingly favored by the smugglers.

The containers arrive in the millions. Only a small number can be inspected. The drugs can easily be mingled with legal cargo or concealed in the walls and doors. The containers are actually tractor-trailers without the wheels and cabs. They usually measure twenty or forty feet long, twelve feet high, and eight feet wide.

Some of the Colombian cocaine was going all the way to Sicily. An indictment returned by a Miami grand jury in November 1989 revealed that the Colombians had established links with the Sicilian Mafia. They were shipping the drug to Sicily through the Caribbean island of Aruba. Once in the hands of the Mafia, the cocaine was distributed throughout Europe.

In 1984 an American pilot named Barry Seal was indicted on drug charges in Florida. He had been employed by the drug bosses for years, flying drugs into the U.S. In hopes of avoiding punishment, he agreed to act as an informant for the Drug Enforcement Administration.

Seal told the DEA that the Colombian chiefs were moving some of their operations to Nicaragua. In June 1984, he proved his credibility by flying 750 kilos of cocaine from Medellín to Las Brasiles airfield, north of Managua, the capital of Nicaragua. On his next flight, scheduled to take him to a Nicaraguan military base, the DEA fitted his plane with hidden cameras.

The result was some excellent shots of Colombian soldiers and Nicaraguans loading the plane with drugs. Seal flew the load as scheduled to Florida. The DEA arranged to seize the drugs in such a way as not to blow Seal's cover.

The DEA hoped to use Seal's high-level drug contacts to track down and capture some of the cartel's top men. Unfortunately, highly placed individuals within the Reagan administration decided to use Seal's information differently. On March 16, 1986, President Reagan showed some of the Seal photos during a TV broadcast and accused "top Nicaraguan officials" of being "deeply involved" in the drug trade.

The DEA agents were shocked. They felt obligated to put out a public statement declaring there was no evidence of top Nicaraguans being implicated in any way.

Seal thought he could safely continue to fly for the drug barons. Their hired killers executed him soon afterward.

By 1988, the amounts of cocaine penetrating into the U.S. had gotten so large that the price kept falling. Up to that time, the Medellín bosses seemed content with their domination of the Florida market. The rival Cali cartel was left to control New York. Now, in order to raise their falling revenues, the Medellín bosses decided to muscle in on New York. The inevitable result was a bloody gang war, marked by exceptional violence on both sides. By the end of the year, estimates of the dead ranged between one hundred and three hundred. There was no end in sight.

The U.S. has tried to persuade the governments of Peru, Bolivia, and other coca-growing countries to reduce coca production by destroying the plants. American material and financial aid goes to programs aimed at uprooting and burning the plants, cutting them down, or killing them by aerial spraying.

The results have been frustrating. The State Department's Bureau of International Narcotics Matters has had to admit that coca production in the Andean region is increasing rapidly. Production doubled, from about 100,000 metric tons in 1988 to about 200,000 in 1989. Where in the 1970s and early 1980s the sale of a few kilos of cocaine or heroin was a big deal, wholesalers these days order and receive thousand-pound lots of cocaine, or as much as 25 tons of marijuana.

The governments of the coca-producing countries are not wholly enthusiastic about helping in the U.S. antidrug effort. Many influential leaders feel that the problem of widespread drug addiction in the U.S. is not their concern. They are also understandably reluctant to give up the sizable revenues that the drug trade brings to their needy treasuries. Finally, they are keenly conscious of the importance of coca income to their own peasants, and they fear that loss of that income could produce potentially revolutionary upheavals.

CARTEL KILLERS

The Colombians are notorious both for their business efficiency and their ruthless violence. In the U.S. they have been known to kill not only their rivals but their rivals' entire families. In one instance, they executed a competitor's wife and eight children aged from two to fourteen and then propped up the whole family in chairs facing the door.

In Colombia they have waged war on public officials. The death toll so far has included a dozen Supreme Court justices, an attorney-general, a minister of justice, a provincial police chief, a crusading antidrug newspaper editor, and hundreds of others.

In 1989, in a phenomenon never seen before, the country's judges briefly went on strike. They demanded special police protection and the right to carry guns and wear bulletproof vests, declaring that they could not carry out their functions in drug cases unless the drug lords' terror campaign against them was brought under control.

The judges' predicament was explained in a World Peace Foundation report. Judgeships were usually assigned to young lawyers at the beginning of their careers. They earned "the equivalent of $90 a month," and received no protection. The drug smugglers would offer them $30,000 to fix or drop a case. "If the judges refuse a third or fourth time, they are killed."

The violence reached a climax in September 1989. At the height of an election campaign, cartel hit men gunned down the leading candidate for the presidency, Senator Luis Carlos Galan. A popular figure who had pledged an all-out war against the drug traffickers, he was regarded as almost certain to win.

President Virgilio Barco reacted swiftly. Thousands of suspects were rounded up in lightning raids. The police seized millions of dollars worth of ranches, farms, planes, boats, and cars. Rewards of up to $250,000 were offered for information leading to the capture of two top traffickers, Pablo Escobar Gaviria and José Gonzalo Rodriguez Gacha.

The president reinstated the extradition process, which the Colombian Supreme Court had declared unconstitutional. In the existing emergency situation, the president used special powers to override the Court. Top drug traffickers who had been indicted in the U.S. would once again be sent there for trial. U.S. Attorney General Richard Thornburgh immediately asked for the extradition of twelve cartel bigwigs.

The first alleged Colombian drug figure extradited under the new rule was Eduardo Martinez Romero. He had been indicted in an investigation involving the laundering of millions in drug money throughout the world. Other top cartel figures soon followed.

The drug lords responded by declaring "total war" against the government. Within a week, a group calling itself the Extraditables took credit for bombing a dozen banks, the offices of the two main political parties, and the leading anti-drug newspaper. The traffickers announced that they would kill ten judges for every man extradited. A new wave of assassinations swept the country.

But the government persisted, and cartel drug operations were seriously disrupted.

The ferocity of the Extraditables only mounted. Hotels,

supermarkets, schools, and a movie theater were bombed in Medellín. In the capital city of Bogotá, cartel agents bombed six schools, a post office, a bank, and a police station 600 feet away from the presidential palace—all within a single weekend. An Avianca airliner was bombed, killing 107 people. A tremendous bomb planted in a car parked in front of police headquarters in Bogotá killed and injured hundreds.

With their demands still unmet, the Extraditables launched a campaign to kidnap members of wealthy families. In a short time they had snatched twenty individuals.

José Gonzalo Rodriguez Gacha was trapped by government forces in December 1989. Gunned down in the shootout that followed, Gacha was the highest-level drug kingpin brought down in Colombia. New waves of antigovernment violence loomed.

Between August 1989 and January 17 the following year, when they declared a truce, the traffickers set off 263 bombs, killing 209 people. The truce lasted about two months. The government refrained from extraditing any drug operators to the U.S. and conducted no further raids. The drug lords controlled their violence.

Then, late in March 1990, extraditions resumed, and a lab raid was announced. The traffickers renewed their war against the government more ruthlessly than ever.

Many Colombians who had enthusiastically supported the antidrug offensive after the assassination of Senator Galan had begun to have doubts. More and more voices were heard urging the government to set up a dialogue with the cartels and work out some sort of mutually acceptable arrangement.

The drug bosses made the government some offers that sounded tempting. They would stop manufacturing and selling cocaine, they said, if the government would leave them to enjoy their wealth in peace. As a good-will gesture in February 1990, they turned over to the government an enormous complex of cocaine-processing laboratories near the border with Panama. It was capable of producing twenty tons of cocaine a month, or one-third of Colombia's estimated total production of 325 tons in 1989.

President Barco scoffed at these offers and vowed to pursue the fight. "We don't think the offer is sincere," said General Miguel Gomez Padilla, commander of the national police force.

For the six weeks following the commencement of President Barco's campaign against the drug lords, shipments of cocaine to the U.S. dropped sharply. But they then returned to the same level as before the government crackdown. The smugglers had found new ways to evade the law.

THE NEW SOUTHWESTERN FRONT

Meanwhile, U.S. efforts to clamp down on the flood of drugs moving into south Florida were achieving good results. The drug lords decided to find new entry channels, though they would not totally abandon the still usable Florida coastline. They did not have far to look.

It was immediately obvious that the 2,013-mile border between Mexico and the southwestern U.S. was ideal for smuggling. Much of it follows the course of the shallow, easily crossed Rio Grande. Vast stretches run through bleak, uninhabited desert terrain. This border has long served as an entryway for tens of thousands of illegal Mexican immigrants. Tons of heroin and marijuana were already crossing it every month, but it had not yet been used for smuggling cocaine on a truly large scale.

Often unguarded at many points, the southwestern border is also well situated as a starting point for moving cocaine into the remotest corners of the American heartland. The traffickers swiftly turned Los Angeles, Tucson, and Phoenix into important distribution centers.

Startling evidence of the scope of cocaine operations in this region came to light in September 1989. Federal agents seized nineteen tons of the drug, plus $12.2 million in cash, in a warehouse in a quiet residential district of Los Angeles. The drug's street value was estimated at from $7 billion to $20 billion. It was by far the biggest drug haul in history.

The warehouse manager told drug agents that sixty tons had passed through the warehouse in the last year, with cash transactions totaling $80 billion.

The lawmen who carried out this historic drug bust were certainly elated by it, but they also had reason to be depressed. The sheer quantity indicated that America's drug problem was even bigger than the most pessimistic previous estimates. The amount seized was at first thought to equal 5 percent of the annual world cocaine production, but more realistic analysis showed that it amounted to considerably less than that.

Shortly after the big bust, a Coast Guard vessel in the Gulf of Mexico seized five tons of cocaine on a freighter. Another five tons were discovered in a Texas farmhouse near the Mexican border. New York then reported its biggest haul ever: six tons of coke hidden in barrels of dangerous chemicals.

Despite such huge seizures, the wholesale price of cocaine in the Los Angeles area remained stable at $21,000 a kilo. Obviously, there was still plenty in the hands of the dealers.

The U.S. had only limited forces to deploy in the southwest. Border Patrol officers in Arizona, for instance, each had to patrol twelve miles of that harsh terrain, and the latest U.S. budget slashed the number of officers even further. To make the smugglers' task still easier, they soon found that some officers could be bribed into looking the other way.

Federal prosecutors contend that one officer yielded to a different kind of temptation. They are investigating a nineteen-year veteran of the Border Patrol, Gary P. Callahan, who was arrested on charges of conspiring to possess and distribute cocaine.

According to the prosecutors, Callahan was patrolling an area of hills and scrubland one night when he encountered eight or ten men with backpacks, crossing the border. He gave chase, and most of them dropped their backpacks. He said he recovered eight packs, each filled with more than forty pounds of cocaine. Callahan claims that he turned in all he found. But the prosecutors insist that he actually hid eighty pounds of the drug and delivered it to a dentist, who has since admitted to being a smuggler. It seems that Callahan was romantically involved with the dentist's sister.

Callahan, described as an enthusiastic and dedicated agent, was suspended without pay. He pleaded not guilty to the charges, but failed to appear at a subsequent hearing. Callahan is currently listed as a fugitive from justice.

In that part of the world, there is never any shortage of *"burros,"* or "mules." These are the men, women, and children who smuggle the drugs into the U.S., most of them carrying the goods on their backs as they trek on foot through the rugged countryside. Some actually do use mules or horses. Mexico's widespread poverty and unemployment insure a constant supply of volunteers for this arduous task.

But many of the carriers are at least middle-class and conceal the drugs in their cars in dozens of clever ways. Best paid of all are the pilots. They can command up to $200,000 a flight in a small twin-engine plane.

"The drug craze has so permeated every part of society that we no longer have a typical profile for a smuggler," said Rudy M. Camacho, Customs Service director of inspection control in Nogales, Arizona. "We've pulled pounds of heroin off grandparents with kids in tow."

Amateur pilots tell of seeing planes land at remote airstrips in the middle of the night. The runways are lighted only by the headlights of a station wagon. The pilot taxis to the end of the runway, throws out the drug package, and takes off without ever coming to a stop. The station wagon picks up the package and roars away into the night.

Vehicles sometimes carry the drugs from Mexico into Texas, Arizona, New Mexico, or California and drive them directly to the dealers. Drugs that get into the U.S. by air or sea are often loaded onto cars and trucks, usually near the border. Some may be transported as far away as New York, as well as to the southwestern distribution centers. Upon delivery, they are repackaged and driven to their final destinations.

A map of the interstate highway system would be virtually identical to a map of the drug smugglers' most frequently used distribution routes. The state police, who patrol these highways, seize only a small fraction of the drugs.

"We're not bragging for a minute," said Sergeant Roy Herren, chief of the intelligence section of the Missouri Highway Patrol. "We know we're barely touching the traffic."

In the mideighties, an estimated one-third of the cocaine smuggled into the U.S. came across the southwestern border. By 1990, U.S. officials had raised their estimate to 70 percent.

The U.S. has stepped up its efforts to seal this border, announcing in March 1990 that a network of radar-carrying balloons would be set up along the southern border to identify drug-carrying planes. But American efforts have been hampered by Mexican reluctance to closely coordinate antidrug campaigns. Ever since the creation in November 1989 of a U.S. antidrug task force under army command, the Mexicans have been alarmed about what they see as U.S. militarization of the border. They have an almost paranoid fear of a possible U.S. invasion.

As Mexican-American relations now stand, it is highly unlikely that Mexico will agree in the foreseeable future to the repeated U.S. request that American planes be permitted to pursue drug-smuggling planes flying from the U.S. into Mexico.

● ● ●

Some of the sources for the heroin and marijuana that enter the U.S. are the same as the sources for cocaine. But most are different, and practically all shipments of these two drugs arrive here via different routes.

3

Heroin and Marijuana International

Heroin is derived from another narcotic, called morphine. Morphine has long been used legally in medical practice as a painkiller. It is refined out of a gummy substance drawn from the opium poppy. One kilo of morphine can be refined from about ten kilos of opium. The morphine can be further refined to produce heroin.

Until the early 1970s, the raw material for most of the heroin consumed in the U.S. came from Turkey. It was refined in laboratories in Marseilles, in southern France. This was the notorious "French Connection." Then the Marseilles operation was exposed and destroyed by U.S. and French police. The U.S. put pressure on the Turkish government, which sharply reduced opium poppy production.

Poppy cultivation soon moved to the "Golden Triangle,"

an area located in remote border regions of Laos, Thailand, and Myanmar (formerly Burma). During the Vietnam War, an estimated one in three American soldiers used heroin originating in this area.

In the late 1970s and early 1980s, another area known as the "Golden Crescent" gradually developed into the primary source. It runs through backcountry areas of Iran, Pakistan, and Afghanistan.

Stepped-up American demand later stimulated a rapid increase in opium cultivation in Mexico, from 21 metric tons in 1984 to 45.55 tons in 1987 and considerably more since then. About a third of this is smuggled into the U.S. in the form of heroin.

More recently the Golden Triangle has regained a strong position in the U.S. market. In 1987 only about 18 percent of the heroin in the U.S. came from the area. Today the figure has climbed to 45 percent.

THE ASIAN PRODUCERS

The Golden Crescent alone produces 1,000 to 2,500 metric tons of heroin a year, mostly in Afghanistan. It provides nearly half the heroin sold in the U.S. and Canada, 80 percent of Europe's supply, and all of Africa's. Much of this product is shipped via Turkey. A substantial quantity is controlled by Nigerians, who move it through Africa.

Some Golden Crescent heroin shipments are smuggled through unexpected channels. Highly placed officials in Pakistan are said to be behind deliveries through a Norwegian connection. Recent arrests of military officers acting as drug couriers may indicate that the Pakistani army is deeply involved.

Still other shipments have been reported going through the Soviet Union and other Eastern European countries. These nations have traditionally denounced the drug trade as a shameful affliction of the Western world. In recent times, however, they have had to report a growing drug problem within their own borders.

The Golden Triangle countries of Laos, Thailand, and Myanmar produce less heroin than the Golden Crescent. Between 2,600 and 3,000 tons of raw opium are currently produced in the Golden Triangle; that is enough for about 300 tons of heroin. But in distribution to the U.S., it has overtaken the Golden Crescent.

Thailand had won the praise of Western governments for sharply reducing its poppy cultivation. But it has, instead, become the main smuggling and shipping center. Most of the area's poppies are now grown in Myanmar and Laos.

For a time much of the Golden Triangle's heroin destined for the U.S. was smuggled through London and Amsterdam by Chinese "triads," or secret societies. A vigorous police effort has recently closed off those ports. The majority of the shipments now move through Thailand as well as Hong Kong.

The triads consist of Chinese living and operating both in Southeast Asia and the U.S. These hard-driving traders are believed to have penetrated U.S. heroin markets formerly controlled by the Mafia.

In the early 1980s, the demand for heroin leveled off in the U.S. and cocaine became more popular. Some of the opium-producing areas were suddenly caught with a surplus of heroin. Particularly in the Golden Triangle, the drug became available at very low prices. The result was a dramatic spread of addiction among these Asian populations, with the inevitable accompaniment of a rise in street crime.

MEXICO MOVES IN

Meanwhile, Mexico was developing as a third source. Mexican heroin, called "brown" because of its dark color, was long regarded as an inferior commodity among American users. But Mexico's share of the U.S. market has grown considerably in recent years as a result of its introduction of a new form of the drug. Called "black tar," this crudely processed but potent heroin is both cheaper and purer than the old familiar "brown."

In the early 1980s, one of the most important Mexican drug cartels had its headquarters in Guadalajara. Its top men had already amassed millions of dollars, all securely deposited in U.S. banks or invested in Sun Belt real estate.

One of these drug lords, Miguel Angel Felix Gallardo, benefited from excellent contacts with the police in the western Mexican states of Baja California and Sonora. He commanded an extensive distribution network throughout the southwestern U.S. Gallardo originally used it to pass heroin but brought in cocaine as well when that drug became popular in the U.S. By 1980 he had a farflung international business empire that included banks, planes, a radio network, and cocaine refineries.

MEXICO'S CORRUPTION PROBLEM

Two Mexican police agencies share responsibility for fighting the drug trade. One is the Direcciòn Federal de Seguridad (Federal Security Directorate), familiarly known as the DFS. The other is the Federal Judicial Police. The latter is regarded by American drug authorities as the more trustworthy of the police agencies.

The DFS is or was quite different. In the provinces, some DFS agents have worked as security guards and strong-arm men for the *narcotraficantes* (drug traffickers). DFS men helped the traffickers move the drugs. Nearly all of the drug kingpins at one time carried DFS credentials, given or sold to them by DFS agents. The DFS allegedly took a fourth of the drug profits.

It was the DFS that had persuaded the *narcotraficantes* to set up their headquarters in Guadalajara and build a narco-industrial complex there. The DFS found houses for them, coordinated operations, protected the drug smugglers against interference by other government agencies, and provided automatic weapons.

The depth of the corruption was illustrated by an incident in 1985. U.S. agents of the Drug Enforcement Administration picked up a radio message ordering a drug mobster to deliver a cash shipment to the Guadalajara airport. Lacking jurisdiction to act inside Mexico, they notified the Mexican police. Thirty Mexican agents converged on the plane while the transfer was underway. But their leader had a private talk with the top drug dealer aboard the plane and allowed it to take off. The DEA men later discovered that the Mexican police officer had received a sizable bribe.

In another incident, a new *comandante* of the Judicial Police got a sudden visit from *narcotraficante* Rafael Caro Quintero and some of his mobsters carrying submachine guns. Quintero spat a brief query at him: "Are you with us?" The *comandante* was furious at the lack of respect and the implied insult. He glared at Quintero. But the *narcotraficante* was not embarrassed. *"¿Qué quieres?"* ("What do you want?") he demanded of the policeman. *"¿Plata, o plomo?"* ("Silver, or lead?") The *comandante* made the "right" choice and lived well after that. His agents have never molested the big traffickers.

Not all Mexican law-enforcement agents are corrupt. Thirty-two were killed during antidrug operations in 1989. Scores of local police officers and soldiers were wounded while assisting them.

Mexican police have racked up some impressive achievements. Cocaine seizures rose from 5.3 metric tons in 1985 to more than 34 tons between December 1, 1988, and December 31, 1989. In the same period, the police destroyed almost 8,500 acres of opium poppy fields and 10,500 acres of marijuana. They confiscated over 600 kilos of heroin and opium paste and over 500,000 pounds of marijuana. More than 11,000 drug offenders were arrested.

Still, for every ton of drugs confiscated, experts estimate that nine get through.

A new Mexican president, Carlos Salinas de Gortari, was elected at the end of 1988. A U.S. State Department report issued three months later praised the new Salinas administration for substantially improved antidrug efforts. The two countries have signed a new agreement on intensified antidrug programs. Drug seizures and arrests in Mexico have risen sharply.

Specially notable was the arrest of Gallardo in April 1989. By that time he had earned the title of "Number 1 narcotics trafficker in Mexico," according to the country's attorney-general. Gallardo was thought to have smuggled as much as two tons of cocaine a month into the U.S. His network of corrupted officials was so large that all 300 men of the police force of his native town, Culiacan, were brought in for questioning hours after his arrest. Several promptly deserted and disappeared rather than face prosecution.

The Mexican drug runners fear and hate the U.S. agents of the Drug Enforcement Administration who are assigned to work in their country. Not only are these zealous agents constantly turning up new evidence, but they also seem stubbornly incorruptible.

Leaders of the drug cartel once became convinced that the only effective way to intimidate the DEA men was to kidnap one of their best and kill him. As we shall see, it was not long before they succeeded.

MEXICAN MARIJUANA STORY

Back in 1977, the U.S. had gotten the Mexican government to agree to start spraying any marijuana plantations, wherever they could be found, with a poisonous herbicide named paraquat. The Mexican growers ignored the obvious danger of allowing these poisoned plants to be put on the market. They harvested the plants and shipped them north. Numerous pot smokers in the U.S. were poisoned, and the resulting nationwide alarm meant at least a temporary halt to sales of Mexican pot in the U.S.

The gap was promptly filled by Colombia's superior product, "Santa Maria Gold," famous among connoisseurs. Colombia was soon supplying some three-fourths of the pot smoked in the U.S., earning an estimated $1 billion a year.

The U.S. had supplied Colombia with a new plane specially designed for spraying crops in mountainous terrain with narrow valleys. This was the Turbo-Thrush, an awkward-looking but efficient plane with a long nose and a bulbous cockpit. The Turbo-Thrush could carry much more fuel and spray than could a helicopter, and it could go higher and faster. It could spray 128 acres a day, while a helicopter could do only 28 acres. The Turbo-Thrush was so effective that by the fall of 1989 there were few marijuana acres left to spray in Colombia.

But the Mexican marijuana planters were producing once again. They specialized in a particular type of marijuana known as sinsemilla. Unlike ordinary pot, sinsemilla has no seeds and is considered the gourmet form of the drug.

The planters had irrigated thousands of desert acres in the state of Chihuahua. They used the most advanced and efficient agricultural techniques. Their vast fields were ridiculously easy to spot from the air, but millions of dollars in well-placed bribe money guaranteed that the Mexican police would ignore them. At the same time, the Mexican government was accepting large sums from the U.S., supposedly for use in the eradication of drug plantations.

DEA agent Enrique (Kiki) Camarena was the first to get word of the tremendous new pot plantations from Mexican informants. Camarena was universally respected as one of the brightest and most courageous of the American investigators. He presented his evidence to the Mexican attorney-general in 1982. That official finally ordered a search-and-destroy raid. Some two hundred tons of sinsemilla were confiscated, along with twenty tons of chemical fertilizer. The men who were running the plantation had been warned of the raid, however, and they got away.

Despite this success, the corruption continued and Mexican marijuana production kept rising. By 1984, pot seizures along the southwestern border of the U.S. had gone up five times since 1980. The Guadalajara traffickers then formed a syndicate to finance the planting of more thousands of acres of sinsemilla. Even some Mexican antidrug officials invested in these plantations.

One *comandante* explained the persistent corruption to DEA investigators: "They make you an offer—'We'll make you wealthy or we'll make you dead.' So you'd rather be wealthy than dead."

DEA agents kept sending reports about the pot plantations to Washington. They pleaded for the U.S. government to bring pressure to bear on the Mexicans to destroy the fields by spraying from the air. The Mexicans were supposedly using American funds to do this, but the DEA men saw little evidence of it.

Concerned about maintaining the U.S.'s "special relation" with the Mexicans, the Reagan administration paid little attention to the DEA reports. Instead, it continued to issue optimistic statements about the Mexican eradication program, based on inflated information provided by the Mexican government.

At last, the DEA agents got permission to fly over the supposedly sprayed fields of marijuana and opium poppies. Their first flights in November 1984 only confirmed their worst fears. The plants were growing abundantly, showing no signs of spraying. A full-scale raid followed, which seized more drugs and drug-making equipment than ever before. *Time* magazine called this raid "the bust of the century."

But subsequent DEA complaints about Mexican corruption fell on deaf ears in Washington. "What's gonna have to happen?" asked Kiki Camarena bitterly in January 1985. "Does somebody have to die before anything is done?"

On February 7, 1985, Camarena walked out of his Guadalajara office and headed for a lunch date with his wife. That was the last time his fellow agents ever saw him alive. Later, when his decomposing body was unearthed, it was clear that he had been gruesomely tortured and mutilated before being put to death.

Rafael Caro Quintero and Ernesto Fonseca Carrillo were arrested and charged with the murder some months later. There followed four years of complicated legal proceedings, but in December 1989 both men were convicted. They were sentenced to life imprisonment. Mexico has no death penalty for capital crimes.

The successful prosecution of two such wealthy and influential drug traffickers was another sign of the determination of Mexico's new president to wage all-out war against the drug lords. U.S. authorities continued the investigation. In January 1990, the former head of Mexico's Federal Judicial Police, Manuel Ibarra-Herrera, and the former head of the Mexican branch of Interpol, Miguel Aldana-Ibarra, were indicted with three others by a Los Angeles grand jury for taking part in the murder of Camarena. It remained unclear whether the Mexican government would extradite these men to the U.S. for trial.

Three months later a physician, Dr. Humberto Alvarez-Machain, was arrested by bounty hunters in Mexico and turned over to U.S. authorities in California. He had already been indicted by the U.S. as an accomplice in Camarena's murder. Alvarez was said to have injected Camarena with stimulants to keep him conscious during his ordeal by torture.

Mexican authorities were outraged by what they viewed as an intrusion on their country's sovereignty. They said the U.S. Drug Enforcement Administration had engineered the arrest and that such arrogance cast doubt on further U.S.-Mexican antidrug cooperation. The DEA has denied any direct involvement.

In August 1990, a U.S. Federal judge ruled that the U.S. had violated its extradition treaty with Mexico by abducting Machain. He ordered that the doctor be returned to Mexico. As of this writing, no final ruling has been announced.

The man regarded as the central figure in the Camarena case was Rubén Zuno Arce, brother-in-law of a former Mexican president. He was the main link between the Guadalajara drug traffickers and corrupt Mexican officials highly placed in law enforcement and military circles. In the words of Assistant U.S. Attorney Manuel Medrano, "He greased the wheels for protection from corrupt law enforcement."

Zuno was convicted in July 1990 in Los Angeles of violent acts related to Camarena's abduction. He faced a possible life sentence.

Despite such efforts, the flow of marijuana, heroin, and cocaine from Mexico into the U.S. has doubled and then redoubled during the late 1980s. One of the most remarkable operations involving Mexican marijuana was conducted by a group of American teenagers from Coronado High School in San Diego, California. Starting in the mid-1960s, they paddled small amounts of the drug from Baja California to San Diego on surfboards. Over the next twenty years they gradually expanded their operation to include the use of radio-equipped fleets of trucks, high-technology off-loading equipment, and yachts equipped with satellite navigational systems. They were handling drugs from Thailand and South America as well as Mexico. At their peak they had accumulated nearly $100 million. The Drug Enforcement Administration finally uncovered their operation and broke it up.

GUATEMALA GETS HOOKED

In 1987, Mexican heroin traffickers moved south into neighboring Guatemala. According to Western diplomats, the Mexicans trained and financed the poverty-stricken local farmers to shift thousands of acres from fruits and vegetables to opium poppy production. With astonishing swiftness, they developed Guatemala into one of the Western Hemisphere's largest opium producers. By 1989, this small country could supply the raw material for a substantial part of the heroin consumed annually by the estimated 500,000 heroin addicts in the U.S.

Opium production is about fifteen times more profitable for the farmers than their best cash crop. Small landowners can earn a hundred dollars an acre a year growing tomatoes, but two thousand dollars an acre with opium poppies.

Most of the heroin base is shipped to Mexico. There it is refined into an estimated five tons of heroin a year, worth about two to five billion dollars in the marketplace.

At the same time, Guatemala was becoming a major refueling and transshipping point for cocaine headed from Colombia to the U.S. The country is ideally located for these uses, halfway between the Colombian laboratories and the U.S. markets. Pilots stopping here can use smaller planes, which are more difficult to detect on radar. By some estimates, as much as 1,100 pounds of cocaine move through Guatemala every week.

The poorly armed Guatemalan army seems unable or unwilling to confront the growers. The U.S. funded eradication programs, but the growers' rapidly growing supply of arms has endangered the sprayer aircraft. The programs have had to be halted, at least temporarily.

At this writing, cocaine, heroin, and marijuana are flowing in great torrents from all of these countries into the apparently insatiable U.S. market. Large amounts are seized at the borders and inside them, but the supply is more than ample. The traffickers continue reaping huge rewards from the needs and desires of American drug users.

4

Drug Money
International

Almost all drug transactions are in cash. As the cash moves from customers to street-level dealers to middle-level distributors to drug kingpins, it builds into enormous amounts. But these hundreds of millions of dollars in "dirty" cash can neither be spent nor invested nor deposited in banks without arousing the attention of the authorities.

In the U.S., for example, any bank deposit of more than $10,000 must be reported to the Internal Revenue Service. The source of the money has to be identified. Obviously, money derived from an illegal source such as drug trafficking would be unacceptable to any law-abiding financial institution.

But so many legitimate transactions involving more than $10,000 are filed every day that the government has difficulty keeping track of them all. In 1975, only about 3,000 such transactions were reported. By 1988, the number had soared to an estimated 5,500,000. The result is that some drug money does get through.

TURNING "DIRTY" MONEY INTO "CLEAN"

The complex process of converting "dirty" drug money into "clean," usable capital is called "laundering." It requires a high level of skill in financial manipulation, plus a thorough understanding of the worldwide banking and financial systems. When bank officers can be corrupted so that they agree to cooperate in laundering operations, the task becomes easier.

The total amount of drug money laundered each year is estimated at a mind-boggling $300 billion. According to cable-TV's business program *Moneyline*, U.S. banks launder one-third of that amount. Nine-tenths of that $100 billion ends up overseas, contributing substantially to the nation's foreign trade deficit.

Authorities have confiscated only a small fraction of the total, as the drug war's largest cash seizure to date shows. This took place in 1989 in Queens and on Long Island, New York. Nearly $20 million in neatly stacked twenty-dollar bills with a few hundreds was discovered in a passenger van. DEA agents arrested eleven people, believed to be members of Colombia's second-most-powerful drug ring, the Cali cartel.

Authorities said the money was about to be shipped out of the country for laundering. Account records found at the scene showed that the cocaine dealers were taking in about $1 million a day.

In the U.S., some $581 million in proceeds from cash

seizures and the sale of impounded property has been deposited in Justice Department accounts. It is being spent on law enforcement.

Sometimes the drug lords run into unexpected problems handling such incredible amounts of currency. One Colombian trafficker had $400 million he wanted transferred to him from California. But the money was hidden in the rather damp basement of a house. By the time he could arrange for it to be moved, it had rotted away.

The drug bosses get some of their profits into legitimate bank accounts through "smurfs." These are go-betweens who carry amounts of less than $10,000 and deposit them inconspicuously in dozens of banks.

In some cases, officials of various governments have been persuaded to cooperate by enacting and enforcing strict bank secrecy laws. They encourage banks that operate in their territory to establish and maintain secret numbered accounts. Such accounts are extremely useful as shelters for drug money.

The drug lords employ financial agents in countries with banks that are willing to cooperate. The agents set up fake corporations as the owners of the secret accounts. Unlimited amounts of drug money are then accepted into them, thus becoming "clean" and perfectly usable. A local lawyer can then simply withdraw any desired amount from the secret account and "loan" it to the drug kingpin.

THE LAUNDERING CENTERS

Until recently, Panama was a leading center for these huge financial transactions. Until the end of 1989, the commander of the Panamanian armed forces and virtual dictator of the country was General Manuel Antonio Noriega. He had been indicted by two Florida grand juries on drug-trafficking and drug-money-laundering charges. In the late 1980s U.S. President George Bush ordered economic sanctions against Panama and exerted diplomatic pressures in an effort to force Noriega out, but the general arrogantly remained in power.

In December 1989, Bush sent an invasion force into Panama. Noriega took refuge in the Vatican embassy. A democratically elected government replaced his dictatorship. Noriega soon surrendered to U.S. authorities. He was flown to Florida, where preparations began for his trial.

Several other Caribbean countries are known to cooperate with the drug smugglers in laundering drug money. The Bahamas and the Cayman Islands are notorious examples. Other places where drug-money laundering has long been done on a large scale include Uruguay, Hong Kong, and the tiny European states of Liechtenstein and Luxembourg.

Switzerland, one of the world's most important banking centers, has had an extensive system of secret bank accounts for many years. It has recently concluded a treaty with the U.S. under which it agrees to supply information about accounts suspected of containing large amounts of drug money.

But Switzerland has no laws against most forms of money laundering. Its secret accounts unquestionably serve as laundries for many millions of dollars in drug money.

In the tiny nation's biggest money-laundering scandal, a prosecutor charged two Lebanese brothers with using Swiss banks to launder as much as $1.3 billion in drug money. The money reportedly came from Colombia, the U.S., Turkey, and elsewhere.

Elisabeth Kopp had been serving as vice president of Switzerland and minister of justice. She reportedly learned that her husband's currency-trading company was the target of a money-laundering investigation. She allegedly warned him to quit his job as company vice chairman. That act laid her open to a possible indictment for violation of official secrecy. Kopp resigned in the spring of 1989, and Switzerland came under increased pressure from other countries to tighten its laws against money laundering.

In September 1989, it was revealed publicly for the first time that Canadian banks have also been laundering enormous amounts of drug money. A report prepared by the U.S. Drug Enforcement Administration and the Royal Canadian Mounted Police said that seizures of large amounts of cash by border authorities have been increasing at a rapid rate.

The 5,500-mile length of the wide-open U.S.-Canadian border, and the huge numbers of cars that cross every day, make detection of illicit cash shipments difficult. Further complicating the situation is the fact that many transactions are carried out electronically between U.S. banks and those in Canada.

In 1989 Canada at last adopted a law permitting officials to freeze suspected assets and have them forfeited if their owners were convicted of money laundering. For the first time, money laundering became a crime in Canada.

In the U.S., a section of the AntiDrug Abuse Act of 1986 requires the State Department to identify any countries with bank secrecy laws. Those that refuse to sign a treaty or make other arrangements similar to the agreement concluded with Switzerland will lose all U.S. aid and assistance.

A major indictment issued in 1988 accused the Bank of Credit and Commerce International, a bank holding company operating worldwide, of transferring drug funds from accounts here and abroad in such a way as to conceal who was actually getting the money. Documents indicated that BCCI earned a tidy 1.5 percent on laundering transactions.

Eighty-five people employed by BCCI in six U.S. cities were charged, nine of them highly placed executives. The $20-billion holding company, ranked as the world's seventh-largest privately owned financial institution, is controlled by powerful Middle Eastern families. It has branches in seventy-three countries, including nine in the U.S. The Panama branch was cited in Senate hearings as a major money-laundering operation used by General Noriega.

The indictments came after a two-year undercover investigation in which Customs Service agents posed as money-laundering experts. They acted as intermediaries for the transfer of a total of $14 million between the bank and the Medellín drug traffickers. The investigation was dubbed "Operation C-Chase," the *C* standing for hundred-dollar bills, or "C-notes."

In January 1990, two principal units of the bank agreed to plead guilty to reduced charges and to forfeit $14 million. The bank further agreed to oversee cash deposits and loans more closely. After a six-month trial, five of the bank's former employees were convicted.

The commissioner of the U.S. Customs Service, William von Raab, has commented in strong terms: "For some international banks, their sleaze factor is higher than their interest rates."

MOVING AGAINST THE LAUNDERERS

In July 1988, the leaders of the free world's seven most industrialized nations (U.S., Japan, Britain, France, West Germany, Canada, and Italy) agreed to form a money-laundering task force. That group met for the first time in September 1989. Its assignment is to formulate a worldwide plan of action aimed at money laundering.

In 1989 the U.S. made the decision to regulate all cash transfers from American banks to foreign ones. For the first time, banks would be required to keep records every time they transfer funds electronically. About $1 trillion is transferred by the banks every day, making it impossible to track drug money amid these huge amounts unless they are registered.

Making the transfers is simple. All the customer has to do is tell his personal computer to order the bank's computer to move some money from one of his accounts to an account abroad.

The Treasury Department has also announced plans for a highly computerized Financial Crimes Enforcement Network. It will collect data from several government agencies on illicit financial transactions, study patterns of illegal money movements, and help develop enforcement strategies.

MONEY LAUNDERING IN THE U.S.

Banks inside the U.S. have also been involved in large-scale laundering. The Treasury Department has recently had to penalize twenty-five U.S. banks for failing to report properly. In a wave of prosecutions in 1985, even the respectable Bank of Boston was among those cited in news stories as having been charged with helping the traffickers to avoid detection while moving many millions of dollars. The bank pleaded guilty only to failing to file the required forms with the government detailing all international financial transactions in excess of $10,000. It paid a fine of $500,000.

Miami, Florida, is the biggest center for laundering operations. One Miami institution, the Bank of Perrine, was actually purchased by a businessman from Medellín who concealed his criminal record on the application to buy the bank. Four others are thought to be controlled by the Medellín cartel. Florida banks regularly report cash surpluses of $6 to $8 billion a year—more than twice as much as any other state banking system.

Some laundering operations in the U.S. have used bribery rather than secret bank accounts. Consider a hypothetical example: A dealer has accumulated several million dollars. But this is "dirty" money, which, of course, he dares not use. He pays a bank officer 2 percent to accept the deposit and "forget" to file an I.R.S. report. The bank then wires the money to a secret account in a foreign bank. The dealer can then "borrow" from the account and use the laundered money freely.

The biggest operation to disguise the origins of drug money ever uncovered by federal agents was announced early in 1989. It used U.S. banks to ship more than $1 billion a year to the Colombian drug lords. Based in Los Angeles, the operation was known as *La Mina* ("The Mine"). Indictments were issued to 127 people.

The money launderers disguised drug profits by mixing them with proceeds from phony business "fronts"—in the form of wholesale and retail gold and jewelry businesses run mostly out of Los Angeles. Through gold purchases and sales that were never made or were made at inflated prices, the cocaine money was deposited in American banks. The banks, as required by law, reported all cash deposits exceeding $10,000—all of which were documented with invoices declaring that the money came from gold and jewelry transactions.

The launderers had chosen their business fronts wisely, since gold and jewelry are traditionally paid for in cash. Once the money was thus "legitimized," it could be wire-transferred to Medellín or Cali cartel accounts. If any doubts arose about these transactions, the operation could defend itself by showing that it did in fact own gold mines in several South American countries.

Some of the profits were invested in American real estate and other valuables. But much of the money eventually wound up in the Panama and Colombia branches of the Banco de Occidente. The bank was indicted on conspiracy charges. It agreed to plead guilty.

Another massive laundering scheme uncovered at the same time required two major investigations spanning four continents and focused finally on a single account at Republic National Bank of New York. Republic is one of the largest and most respected banks in the U.S. The bank itself, however, was not a target of the investigation.

One of the laundering investigations was code-named Operation Polar Cap. It went after Colombian cocaine money. The cash was allegedly laundered through another Los Angeles wholesale jewelry firm named Ropex, which paid it out in return for nonexistent gold shipments.

Operation Polar Cap scored a major victory in April 1990 when it obtained a court order freezing hundreds of bank accounts in 173 banks, more than half of which were in New

York and Florida. The accounts were suspected of concealing nearly $400 million in Colombian drug profits. Review of the bank records would reveal for the first time how the Medellín cartel conducted its day-to-day business in the U.S. The banks were unaware of the nature of the accounts and have not been accused of any wrongdoing.

"The cartel needs these secret U.S. accounts in order to run their illegal business here," said U.S. Attorney-General Richard Thornburgh. "The massive scope of the cocaine trade in the U.S. requires large amounts of capital."

The other investigation, still a classified secret, implicated the Bulgarian government. It targeted heroin profits from Turkey and the Middle East.

Interestingly, even while millions in illicit funds were moving through the Republic account, authorities found that the bank itself was an innocent party. As soon as the investigation began, the bank cooperated with investigators.

A very different kind of laundering operation is provided by many of the small inner-city businesses that recent and illegal immigrants use to send money abroad. Many of these storefront money-transmitting and check-cashing businesses are sending billions of dollars to drug dealers in South America and Asia.

A small percentage are licensed and legitimate, and these provide a useful service. But most are unlicensed, illegal, and unregulated. The largest numbers of the lawbreakers do business in New York, Florida, Texas, and California. These states have so few regulators, and the number of illicit operations has grown so rapidly in recent years, that their sheer number overwhelms the regulators.

The illicit operations take in large sums in cash from drug dealers, often in suitcases, cartons, and shopping bags.

They also defraud legitimate customers by failing to send their money to its intended addressee. Many of these customers cannot complain to the authorities, because they are either illegal immigrants or recent arrivals in the U.S. who are unfamiliar with the law.

The storefront businesses look very much like banks, with tellers working behind bulletproof glass. "Most of them provide the service of sending fifty dollars back to your grandmother in South America," said Bonnie Klapper, a federal prosecutor in Brooklyn. "But on the side, they make a lot more by charging more for their drug customers."

Their laundering operations are not hard to follow. First, they accept a drug customer's cash. They deposit it in a legitimate bank, usually under the name of a fictitious corporation. The bank transfers the money electronically to another bank, leaving no trace of the real depositor. Most of the money ends up in the hands of the Medellín or Cali drug lords.

SPENDING IT

In Colombia, newly rich drug barons in the early years of their dazzling prosperity were unsure as to how they were expected to behave. They tended at first to invest in showplace homes, luxury cars, expensive jewelry, and the sophisticated weapons needed to protect their ill-gotten wealth. Eventually they turned to the purchase of vast estates, sometimes as places to hide, but also as safe investments. Many of them thus became proud members of the aristocratic class of large landowners. The drug lords are estimated to have placed some $5.5 billion in Colombian real estate.

5

Cocaine
and Crack U.S.A.

A single inescapable fact stands out in any discussion of America's drug epidemic: Americans are currently spending billions on illegal drugs. Estimates of the exact total are, at best, educated guesses and range across a wide spectrum, from $10 billion a year to $80 billion, $100 billion, or even $150 billion. But the exact amount hardly matters. What matters is that it is an enormous sum. With profits of that size available for the taking, it's not surprising that drug dealers are busy in every corner of the land.

COCAINE PROFITS

Cocaine is believed to go through at least six stages (sales and resales) from its arrival to its final sale on the street. It may be "cut" (diluted) with white powders of varied and dubious origin at each stage. The price rises every time the drug moves to a new dealer. In 1987, it sold for an estimated $12,000 to $40,000 a kilo at the first stage. By the time it reached the street it was selling for $80 to $100 a gram (1/1000 of a kilogram). That translates to about $80,000 to $100,000 a kilo.

Interestingly, these seemingly inflated prices actually represented a sharp drop. In 1985, cocaine peaked at $55,000 a kilo. The price fell steadily in following years, despite continually rising demand and mounting losses caused by U.S. law enforcement. The reason? Growing supply. As the traffickers became more experienced, more of their product was getting through.

Then in June 1990, Drug Enforcement Administration officials noted that the wholesale price of cocaine had been rising sharply for about six months. In New York and Los Angeles, prices soared by more than 40 percent. At the same time, heavily diluted cocaine was flooding the market, suggesting that supplies of the drug were dwindling.

"We're not quite sure," said Terence M. Burke, acting head of the DEA, "but it's our hope and belief that there's a good possibility that this has been because of law-enforcement action."

THE ENCOURAGING NUMBERS AND
THE DEPRESSING ONES

Besides the direct cost of the drugs themselves, there are hidden costs as well. These had mounted to about $60 billion by the end of 1989. That constituted a rise of $10 billion since 1985. The steep rise was largely due to increased medical costs for drug addicts, addicted AIDS patients (especially newborn infants), and victims of drug-related crime, as well as the expense of expanding law-enforcement efforts.

The scope of the epidemic was such as to place narcotics "with America's major industries, right up there with consumer electronics, automobiles, and steelmaking," according to Harvard political economist Robert B. Reich. But he added that

> *the narcotics industry doesn't have a net effect of creating wealth. It makes us all substantially poorer. In fact, it is like a reverse industry, tearing things down rather than producing anything.*

Presenting accurate statistics about our drug habit has become more complicated than it used to be. A series of recent surveys has reported contradictory trends.

A 1989 survey by several federal government agencies seemed to show that illegal drug use in the U.S. had declined sharply since 1985. Where 37 million people had used marijuana, cocaine, or other drugs excluding heroin at least once during 1985, only 28 million did so in 1988. That seemed to indicate a dramatic drop of nearly 25 percent.

The survey reported an even sharper drop among "current cocaine users"—those who used it at least once during the month before the survey. This category fell from 5.8 million to 3.9 million, a drop of one-third.

But these optimistic results ran counter to another finding of the same survey: hard-core users of cocaine or crack—those who snorted or smoked the drug once a week or more—*increased* by one-third, from 647,000 to 862,000.

The survey's reliability was undermined by its failure to cover certain classes of people, such as prisoners, other institutionalized persons, and the homeless. These groups include large numbers of drug abusers. Nor did it inquire into another of the largest categories, heroin users. Many of these are dependent on cocaine as well.

Almost certainly, the survey also reflected a good deal of underreporting. An unknown number of the individuals polled were probably afraid or unwilling to admit that they used drugs. This is a problem in all drug surveys. Otherwise the survey's figures would unquestionably have been higher.

In 1985 there were an estimated 12 million cocaine users. Though the count in the 1989 survey was lower, users were revealed to be snorting cocaine or smoking crack more frequently. Of those surveyed, 11 percent used the drug once a week or more in 1988. Four percent did so daily.

Two groups increased their use of cocaine and crack: African-Americans and Hispanics.

New figures were released by the National Institute on Drug Abuse (NIDA) in December 1990. The NIDA report showed a significant decrease in the number of hard-core cocaine abusers in the nation, from 860,000 in July 1989 to 662,000 in December 1990. "Our hard work is paying off," President Bush commented.

But these figures were challenged by Senator Joseph Biden, chairman of the Senate Judiciary Committee, who said the NIDA survey "misse[d] more drug addicts than it counted." The Senate Judiciary Committee's own findings indicated that the number of hard-core cocaine users in the country had *increased* significantly—from 2.2 million in May 1990 to 2.4 million in December 1990. This report did factor in high-risk groups such as prisoners and the homeless.

In 1990, Dr. Louis W. Sullivan, secretary of Health and Human Services, reported a 20 percent drop in cocaine-related hospital emergency-room admissions in the fourth quarter of 1989. "We are making significant headway," he exulted, "in our efforts to establish a drug-free America." Surveys compiled that year showed that the number of cocaine users had fallen to at least 8 million, including about 2.2 million frequent or heavy users.

But a 1990 U.S. Senate report left the public confused as to whether optimism was justified. It stated that cocaine abuse was more than twice as high as previous estimates, with 1 American in 100 using the drug weekly. In Washington, D.C., the rate was said to be a startling 1 in 30, while New York City's rate was 1 in 40.

The National Parents' Resource Institute for Drug Education (PRIDE) got some intriguing results in 1989 when it surveyed high-school seniors who have used cocaine. Two-thirds were male. Two out of three smoked marijuana daily or weekly. About 43 percent had first smoked marijuana at age eleven or younger. Sixty percent had drunk beer at age thirteen or earlier.

Another survey of high-school seniors was released in February 1990 by the Institute of Social Research of the University of Michigan. It showed that narcotics use was still a grave problem, with 50.9 percent of those questioned admitting they had tried an illicit drug during 1989. The figure did, however, represent a decline of 3 percent from the previous year and almost 6 percent from 1987.

The marijuana figures were striking. Only 17 percent said they had used the drug during the previous thirty days, compared to 37 percent in 1979.

Even this careful study left some blanks. It did not cover high-school dropouts. There is considerable evidence that drug abuse among this group, especially abuse of crack, is half again as large as for the seniors—and rising. Dropouts were believed to comprise more than 27 percent of young men of the age of high-school seniors.

Like the other surveys, this one showed no significant reduction in crack use.

A ROTTEN BUSINESS

Much of the drug crack is used in so-called crack houses. These can be found in apartments, hotel rooms, or abandoned buildings.

Dealers seeking to prevent raids by rival dealers or law-enforcement authorities sometimes fix up their crack houses so that they are veritable fortresses. They have reinforced steel doors and full-time armed security guards. The sales of crack and collection of the money are conducted by means of safe drawers that slide back and forth through the doors or walls. The armed guards are often youngsters; their age and lack of experience with weapons help account for the recent increases in the number of wild shootouts and killings in the streets.

Few if any of the dealers ever make the big money they thought they would. Instead they discover they've taken on a round-the-clock job, six or seven days a week. Customers show up at all hours of the day or night.

The dealers get fifty cents for every five-dollar vial of crack they sell. Their pay is often docked if they arrive late or quit early. They may get shot or badly beaten if their bosses even suspect they're trying to cheat. In East Harlem the typical penalty is getting one's kneecaps shot out. One drug distributor shows his dealer-employees a jar full of teeth, which he says he yanked out of the mouths of would-be cheaters. Younger helpers who work as lookouts may earn as little as twenty or thirty dollars a day—paid out of the dealers' earnings.

The average street career of the dealers lasts between three and six months. By the end of that time they're either in jail, badly maimed, or dead. As one ex-dealer told the *New York Times,* "A lot of my friends, buddies, people I knew, they took them out in a box or they were taken by the police."

Yet there is never a shortage of recruits. The myths about the sky-high incomes, the big cars, flashy clothes, and easy women persist despite the grim reality that is there on the streets for all to see. "I wanted that glamorous life," said another ex-dealer, "and it seemed like that was the only way to get it."

Even the rare dealer who does take in large amounts of cash doesn't hang on to much of it. He has to keep up a dazzling front to earn the respect of his rivals, his customers, and the neighborhood in general. That absorbs the profits.

Many dealers either use the drugs they are supposed to be selling or buy drugs with the money they earn. An admission often heard from the few who managed to get out runs like this: "I never made any money. I was my own best customer."

In New York City, dealers have been operating increasingly out of restaurants, grocery stores, automobile-parts shops, and other seemingly legitimate businesses. Some are fully functioning businesses; others do very little legal business. But their working fronts make them harder to detect and put out of operation.

"It has to be the height of ridiculousness," said Captain Stephen Nasta of the N.Y. Police Department, "for someone to be able to go into a store and buy fresh bread and milk and cocaine." When the authorities do manage to close down a disguised dealership, the dealer can all too easily move to another location down the block and reopen for business.

FROM THE POOR TO THE WELL-TO-DO

The vast majority of crack addicts has been concentrated for nearly a decade in the inner-city ghettos. Until recently they were almost all poor and members of minority groups.

But new studies show that crack addiction has spread alarmingly among the white middle and upper classes. Oddly, these groups are the same ones that show up in surveys as reducing their occasional and recreational use of powdered cocaine. When it comes to crack, they are proving no more able than ghetto residents to resist its potent lure—with its inevitable accompaniment of rapid addiction.

According to Dr. Arnold Washton, a widely respected expert on the drug epidemic and director of a New York treatment clinic, there are now more crack addicts among white middle-class people than any other segment of the population.

"These new addicts," Washton told the *New York Times,*

are business executives and house painters and doctors and receptionists. And if you met them on the street or at the Little League game, you wouldn't have a clue they're smoking their brains out on crack back home in the basement.

The typical middle-class addict is a white male in his thirties or forties. He is intelligent, and at least in the early phases of his addiction he is employed. He is married, though his marriage may be shaky because of his habit. He is probably addicted to several substances at once, such as crack, alcohol, and marijuana.

The epidemic does not affect only males, however. The considerable number of middle-class women addicted to crack is rising fast.

Occupations with long hours fraught with nervous tension mixed with boredom are most likely to produce crack and cocaine addicts. Such jobs include air-traffic controllers, pilots, nuclear-plant workers, ambulance drivers, doctors, nurses, bus and taxi drivers, policemen, and firefighters. The temptation is strong also for people whose jobs entail long, frequent, lonely travel, or who face fierce competition. Notable among this group are professional athletes and entertainers.

These more affluent addicts tend to be more secretive about their drug habit than are poorer ones. They probably feel that they have more to lose in property, income, and reputation. Three facts about cocaine and crack make it easy for employed persons to use either of them at work: Both can be carried in a small vial or aspirin bottle; they can be taken quickly and their effect is almost instantaneous; and they don't require much equipment.

People who are high on crack or cocaine tend to think

themselves capable of normal or even superior work. They feel more confident and charming and wittier than usual in their relations with others. They are convinced that no one can notice their drugged condition. Where other drugs such as heroin make it difficult for addicts to function at all, low to moderate doses of cocaine can actually improve performance—for a short while. Difficult tasks seem easier, and boring ones can be done more quickly.

Actually, cocaine impairs eye-hand coordination. A study published in January 1990 showed that almost one of every four drivers between sixteen and forty-five who were killed in New York City traffic accidents in recent years tested positive for cocaine.

Middle-class addiction carries certain hidden costs to society. One of these is the devastating effect on families of a breadwinner's addiction. As crack drains away the family's income, savings, and other assets, often costing the addict his job, formerly stable and secure families fall apart.

There is also the cost to the nation's economy. In a survey of state governors, mayors of large cities, and chief executives of the nation's 1,000 biggest corporations, nearly 80 percent said that substance abuse was a significant problem in their organizations. Employers reported that from 6 to 15 percent of their work force had an alcohol or addiction problem.

The General Motors Corporation, for example, estimates that addiction among its workers costs the company more than $1 billion annually in absenteeism and treatment programs. In the year before a worker seeks treatment, the average GM worker-addict barely makes it to work half the time.

Dr. Robert G. Wiencek, director of GM's occupational

safety and health program, declared that "the individual who is using cocaine is unsafe. He uses very poor judgment." Heavy users often get deep into debt, and they may embezzle company funds to pay off drug debts. They may accept bribes or kickbacks, and sometimes they become targets for blackmail.

Otto Jones is head of Human Affairs International, which designs employee assistance programs for insurers and employers. According to Jones,

> *Drug users will incur 300 percent more medical costs, on average, than the rest of a company's employees. The users lose twice as much work as the average employee and are five times more likely to be involved in accidents off the job.*

Middle-class crack or cocaine users often start out using only occasionally, for "recreational" purposes. They may use only on social occasions, sharing the fun with friends, or on weekends. But statistical studies have shown that at least two out of ten will become addicted.

Many businesses have set up employee assistance programs to provide treatment and counseling for addicted employees. They may emphasize primary prevention, with wellness programs, stress management, and employee welfare. Secondary prevention programs focus on early identification and treatment of troubled employees. Some provide telephone hotlines, information and evaluation clinics, or referrals to treatment facilities.

A newly enacted law, the Drug-Free Workplace Act, requires thousands of companies that have federal contracts to adopt antidrug policies. Many large corporations provide space for regular meetings of Alcoholics Anonymous or Narcotics Anonymous.

Employee assistance programs are currently available to about 20 million workers. That is three times more than in 1983, the year the crack epidemic started. About the same number of jobholders are believed to be illicit drug users. Many use more than one drug, and these multiple users are particularly difficult to treat. Of all the causes of death due to drugs, long-continued multiple use is rated as the biggest killer.

According to James E. Burke, chairman of the strategic planning committee at the medical supply company Johnson & Johnson,

The workplace is an easier place to deal with drugs than any other place. You have more control, and you can build a supportive environment, which is sometimes difficult to do in the community.

Richard Lesher, president of the U.S. Chamber of Commerce, believes the paycheck is the employer's "most effective weapon in the war against drugs. If you and I believe that our jobs are contingent on our being drug-free, it creates a powerful incentive."

Few of the administrators running employee assistance programs report good results. Most see little improvement either in absenteeism or productivity.

But there was at least one encouraging sign. It was contained in a July 1990 report by a company that conducts many of the drug tests done for employers. SmithKline Beecham Clinical Laboratories reported that the number of workers and job applicants who have tested positive for drug use has declined since 1987. In that year 18.1 percent tested positive, while in the first six months of 1990 only 13.8 percent did.

THE MOUNTING COSTS

One way to get a clearer grasp of the costs of the drug war is by comparing it with the Vietnam War. Where that military conflict cost America an average of $15 billion a year, the direct costs of the drug war to the government are coming close: they have already reached $10 billion a year. Adding in lost productivity and the "hidden" social costs mentioned at the beginning of this chapter, the annual bill totals more than $60 billion. As journalist Edward Barnes put it in the September 1989 issue of *Life* magazine, "There are no dollar figures for the destruction of neighborhoods or the loss of a generation of children."

Barnes's article also compared Vietnam casualties with those of the drug war. During the worst week of the war, in May 1968, 502 U.S. servicemen were killed. On the drug scene, fatal overdoses and narcotics-related murders average about 450 a week. But if one also takes into account the hundreds of AIDS fatalities that are drug-related, plus the deaths of children due to neglect and abuse by addicted parents, "the death rate exceeds that of Vietnam at its worst."

The worsening crisis demonstrates the unique power of crack, according to J. Michael Walsh of the National Institute on Drug Abuse. Crack, he says,

> has made addicts out of people at a much more rapid rate. [It may take] ten to twelve years for an alcoholic to become dysfunctional [unable to work]. But we are seeing people who have been using crack-cocaine for short periods of only six to eight weeks who are unable to get up and go to work.

INTO THE HEARTLAND

The crack plague has not only been spreading upward through America's social structure. It has also been spreading geographically, from the urban areas to the suburbs and more recently out into America's heartland of smaller towns and countryside.

In New York City's relatively affluent suburbs on Long Island, crack selling and buying has long been common in the poorer areas. Then middle-class whites began coming into these areas to make buys. Today middle-class demand has grown to such proportions that dealers market their wares on the streets of well-to-do communities.

The sellers are largely local working-class youngsters, who see the crack trade as a way to make easy money. "They can go to college," explained Lieutenant Richard A. Franzese of the Suffolk County, Long Island, Narcotics Squad,

and maybe when they're done they can make themselves $25,000 or $30,000 a year. They can go out on the corner and make themselves $1,500 a week tax-free.

A 1989 U.S. Department of Justice report revealed that organized drug mobs have expanded their operations into largely rural states long regarded as virtually drug-free, such as Iowa, Wyoming, Georgia, and South Carolina. The mobs have established distribution networks in the Midwest and rural South. They are dealing cocaine, heroin, marijuana, and synthetic drugs like LSD and methamphetamine. The report named forty-three organized-crime groups trafficking in drugs across the country.

Towns infected by the crack plague include some that

formerly ranked among America's most law-abiding and tranquil. Consider Fort Wayne, Indiana, as an example. It was once known as "the City of Churches." Today an estimated seventy crack houses are in full swing there. Law-enforcement people have dubbed it "the crack capital of Indiana."

Many small towns and rural areas suffer from high unemployment, widespread poverty, and a poorly educated work force. Such conditions make their inhabitants easy targets for a cheap and highly addictive drug like crack. Crime rates are rising faster in some rural counties than in the cities. Law-enforcement officials say that crack addicts, desperate for money to support their habit, are largely to blame.

The infection has been spread mainly from two sources. First, the Jamaican "posses" or gangs active along the East Coast saw opportunities in rural areas and seized them. Their 10,000 to 25,000 members are organized into groups ranging from twenty-five to several hundred. They are believed to control 35 to 40 percent of the nation's crack network.

The Jamaicans were active in the marijuana trade in the 1970s. They got most of their supplies from the crop grown on their home island. When crack became popular in the mideighties, they moved in on it. They got the raw material—powdered cocaine—from the Colombian cartels. The Jamaicans converted it into crack themselves. They soon controlled the East Coast crack trade from the wholesale level all the way down to the street. Most are illegal aliens.

The federal government scored its first conviction of a posse boss in late 1989. Delroy (Uzi) Edwards was convicted in New York on forty-two counts of racketeering, six murders, seventeen assaults, a kidnaping, and a maiming. He was notorious for mistreating and cheating even the members of his own posse, the Rankers. Fourteen of them testified against him.

The Rankers were by no means the largest or the most powerful of the posses. That distinction was reserved for the much bigger gang called the Shower. Nevertheless, the prosecution successfully described Edwards as the ruthless overlord of a Brooklyn crack empire that had expanded into Washington and Philadelphia. In 1987, its peak year, it took in $100,000 a week.

Like the Colombians, the Jamaican dealers are both highly efficient and terrifyingly violent. New York City, Washington, D.C., Miami, and other cities have seen wholesale murders carried out by them execution-style. Federal authorities say the Jamaicans were responsible for 1,400 murders between 1985 and 1988.

An example of their shrewd business sense is the "working fifty," a method of discounting the price of crack to dealers. They offer a rock that is slightly larger than the standard fifty-dollar size. The buyer can smoke some and still sell the rest for the full price.

The Jamaican dealers were not slow to discover that a vial of crack selling for five dollars in New York could bring fifteen dollars in Kansas City. As they developed their networks to take advantage of new high-profit areas, they used every available means of transportation to move their drugs: AMTRAK, commercial airlines, buses, Federal Express, United Parcel Service. Rental cars were a favorite choice. They liked to employ overweight women, who could comfortably hide one- or two-pound drug packages on their persons.

The Jamaicans avoided cities with solidly entrenched gangs of their own, such as Newark, St. Louis, and Chicago. Here business was brisk in heroin and cocaine, and the established mobs were fiercely determined to keep the crack invaders out.

Where the Jamaicans did decide to muscle in on rival mobs, they acted in a blaze of gunfire. Usually they relied on their sizable stocks of Uzi submachine guns and AR-13 assault rifles.

The second source of infection for the American heartland has been two Los Angeles gangs, the Crips and the Bloods. These fast-growing and ambitious groups first won control of the drug trade in southern California. Then they expanded up the West Coast as far as Seattle. Since then they have set up coast-to-coast "franchise" networks second only to those of the Jamaicans. They operate with more than 10,000 gang members in some fifty cities.

Like the Jamaicans, the Los Angeles gangs rely on limitless violence when they run into opposition. So far, conflict has not yet broken out between the East and West Coast gangs. They seem to be dividing the country between them.

BIG-CITY BATTLEGROUNDS

In Kansas City, the Jamaicans were in control until a determined law-enforcement campaign broke their power and drove them out. The city barely had time to congratulate itself before the Bloods and Crips moved in. Today crack is as available in the profitable Kansas City market as it ever was.

With the big gangs often warring against local dealers, and with the locals often warring among themselves, whole sections of at least a dozen major cities have become urban battlefields sometimes described as "dead zones." Police officers avoid these. Ambulances, firefighters, and utility workers often request police escorts if they venture in at all. Residents trapped in such areas feel as if they were living in a no-man's land.

Many of these zones have nicknames, like the Graveyard in Miami, the War Zone in Dallas, or the Wild Wild West district in Baltimore.

Police forces have responded by forming elite units, such as Atlanta's Red Dog outfit and New York's Tactical Narcotics Teams (TNT). These are specially trained and equipped to carry out "sweeps" of the war zones and clean them up through mass arrests of dealers. Most residents appreciate the cleanups, but some complain that they don't last long. The elite units move on to other problem areas and the dealers soon return.

Heightened antidrug police operations have their cost. Fourteen officers were killed in drug-related incidents across the nation in 1988, the largest number on record. In the previous year, eight officers died in this line of duty.

SOCIETY IN A STATE OF SIEGE

The crack invasion has brought with it a crime wave bigger and bloodier than any in our history. Even the tommy-gun wars of the fabled Prohibition era were mere skirmishes by comparison. More than half the males arrested in nine cities in 1988 tested positive for cocaine. In Washington, D.C., the figure was 59 percent, while in New York it exceeded 80 percent. Police there classified one-third of all murders and two-thirds of all robberies and burglaries as drug-related.

Crack brought on its own brand of violence. In the words of a May 1989 *New York Times* editorial,

Crack is distributed by younger, wilder, more heavily armed gangs [than other drugs]. They arrogantly intimidate whole communities and make war on each other to control the lucrative business. In community after community, crack violence has overwhelmed law enforcement.

But it is not the chemical effects of cocaine and crack that cause the violence. A recent study of drug-related homicides in New York showed that 87 percent of those involving cocaine or crack were caused by disputes among dealers rather than by out-of-control addicts. In fact, only 7.5 percent of the killings were due to the behavioral effects of any drug. And two-thirds of those cases involved alcohol, not any form of cocaine.

A recent trial of a crack overlord in Washington, D.C., demonstrated the fear engendered by these especially violent gangs. Rayful Edmond was on trial on a charge of wholesaling cocaine and crack to dealers throughout the nation's capital.

Judge Charles Richey, presiding over the trial, ordered that the jurors' identities be kept secret. Even the judge and the lawyers for both sides were not told their names. Then the judge experimented with putting up vertical venetian blinds to shield the jury from the audience's view. The public was already separated from the proceedings by bulletproof glass panels.

Judge Richey explained his actions by saying that court spectators had been glaring at the jurors, partly to identify and partly to intimidate them. If the jurors were to perform their duties, the judge said, they must be protected.

Edmond was convicted and sentenced to two terms of life in prison without possibility of parole.

OUR JAM-PACKED PRISONS

To cope with the tidal wave of crime and violence, the nation has been forced to spend as never before for police, prosecutors, courts, and judges. An aroused public has forced legislators to toughen the antidrug laws and lengthen prison sentences for drug offenders. The inevitable result has been that jails across the country are monstrously overcrowded.

The state prison population in the U.S. is growing at a rate of 900 inmates per week, the equivalent of two new prisons opening weekly. The total population in the state prisons at the end of 1989 was estimated at 610,000. There were 300,000 more inmates in local jails and about 50,000 in federal prisons. The U.S. would soon have an incredible 1 million persons incarcerated, a record unmatched in any other country.

The emphasis on stepped-up arrests and severe punishments for drug offenders has filled the prisons with drug abusers. Inevitably, drug abuse in prison has risen to a point where it is virtually beyond control. Estimates of drug-abusing prisoners range from 40 to 90 percent.

Drug treatment and rehabilitation programs have barely begun to function behind prison walls.

With drugs selling in prison for three times their street value, corruption of prison staffs has been widespread. Rising numbers of correctional officers have been snared in drug-smuggling and selling operations.

But the principal carriers of drugs into prisons are the visitors who come flooding in to spend a few hours with the convicts. They have developed innumerable ways to deliver the drugs. They bring them in book bindings, on the backs of stamps, inside a girlfriend's bra or a baby's diaper, even stuffed into rectums or vaginas. One popular method is to exchange a drug-packed balloon during a kiss. Visitors can be searched only if there are reasonable grounds for suspicion.

In state after state, prison authorities are under court order to reduce the number of prisoners or find suitable new spaces for them. Millions of dollars have been appropriated for building new facilities or expanding existing ones. But the rate of convictions, a high proportion of them drug-related, is growing so fast that even when the new facilities are completed they will already be overfilled.

Some states have adopted early release of prisoners as a way of making room for the constant stream of new inmates. This would seem to be only a temporary stopgap measure, however. Early release, with criminals getting their sentences arbitrarily reduced by many months, makes a mockery of the criminal justice system. Police officers who dedicate their lives to apprehending these criminals, and the prosecutors who fight to get them convicted, feel that this "solution" to the problem is little more than a bitter joke.

President Bush recently pledged $1.6 billion for the building of 24,000 new federal prison cells, largely for drug violators. Even with these additions, federal penitentiaries will be overcrowded by 25 percent.

PREGNANT ADDICTS

One of the most disheartening aspects of the epidemic is its effects on pregnant women. More than 375,000 infants were born to drug-addicted mothers in 1988, with the total rising fast. Increasing numbers of these women were crack addicts. In New York City alone, the number of crack-addicted babies doubled between 1986 and 1987, rose by 70 percent in 1988, and rose again by the same amount in 1989. It added up to about 5 percent of all live births in the city.

Crack children are at great risk of parental abuse. The drug seems to spur some people to uncontrollable violence. The result has been a sharp rise in the number of cases of crack-crazed battering of children. In one widely cited case, a five-year-old girl was found dead with a broken neck, a broken arm, large circular welts on her buttocks, and cuts and bruises on her mouth. Her brother, nine, was found the next day, huddled in a closet. Both his legs were fractured, he had eight other broken bones, and bruises covered his body.

Pregnant women who use crack endanger not only their own lives but those of their babies as well. Many are born abnormally tiny, with brain damage and physical deformities. Each of these children requires intensive hospital care that runs up an average total bill of $90,000. The total cost figure for their treatment in the U.S. currently amounts to $2.5 billion.

Young women addicted to crack commonly sell their bodies as prostitutes to obtain money for the drug. Almost unbelievably, in some families their own mothers and brothers obtain sex partners for them. Some teenage girls have abandoned their families and formed violent new criminal gangs to get the money they need. For the first time, female users have begun to outnumber males in some neighborhoods.

Equally depressing are recent statistics on arrests of teenagers of both sexes. In New York City alone, arrests of thirteen- and fourteen-year-olds for the possession and sale of heroin and cocaine (almost always crack) doubled in the single year from 1986 to 1987 and then redoubled the following year. The steep increase showed that adult dealers were using more and more children to sell drugs to other children. The dealers know that the penalties are far less severe in family court, which handles cases involving youths up to the age of fifteen. Older teens face tougher treatment in adult criminal courts.

Crack patients are an aggravating problem even while under hospital treatment. They often sneak out of their beds to buy crack on the street and smoke it in their rooms. They commonly steal from the hospital and other patients. Under the drug's influence, they frequently assault hospital personnel.

Whatever the evil influences of other drugs such as marijuana and heroin, they cause less violence by their abusers. Those two drugs have spread through the U.S. by paths different from those followed by cocaine and crack.

6

Marijuana and Heroin U.S.A.

Marijuana is the easiest to grow and process of all the drugs derived from plants. Its scientific name is *Cannabis sativa*. It will thrive in almost any conditions and almost anywhere. The plant is also known as hemp, and until the late nineteenth century it was commonly made into a sturdy cloth that was used in sails, rope, cordage, and even clothing.

Unlike cocaine or heroin, marijuana requires no refining. The active ingredient, THC (delta-9-tetrahydrocannabinol), resides in the leaves and flowers. These need only be harvested and dried, and can then be smoked.

To obtain the more powerful drug hashish from the resin of the marijuana plant, only a simple refining process is required. Hashish is sold in smokable cakes, or in an oil that can be smoked with tobacco. It is five to eight times stronger than marijuana.

MARIJUANA COMPLEXITIES

As noted earlier, the use of marijuana in the U.S. has declined since the late 1970s. Nevertheless, pot is still the most popular of all the illicit drugs. Estimates of the number of occasional users—those who use it at least once a year—range from 20 to 40 million.

These statistics would seem to show how ineffectual the antimarijuana laws have been. In 1937, when the federal law banning marijuana was passed, there were only an estimated 50,000 pot smokers.

Arnold S. Trebach, a professor at American University in Washington, D.C., and director of the Drug Policy Foundation, estimates the number of those who smoke pot daily at about 3 million. Trebach believes that about half of these are compulsive smokers, who would experience discomfort if they tried to stop. If his estimates are accurate, about one in twenty users is truly addicted.

The majority of pot smokers are in their teens or early twenties. Frequent smokers tend to be unmotivated and inattentive. Marijuana interferes with memory formation and distorts the smoker's sense of time and space. Students who use it often cannot remember what has just been said in class, or they remember it only in twisted form. The stoned student has difficulty mastering new knowledge.

Professor Trebach is one of those who challenge the conventional emphasis on pot's hazards. He points out that there are large numbers of teenagers who limit their pot smoking to evenings and weekends, use moderate amounts, and never become addicted. They manage to meet life's challenges and function responsibly. Trebach argues that for some youngsters, pot can be helpful in coping with stress.

Some medical authorities contend that marijuana is more harmful to the respiratory system than tobacco and that frequent users run a higher risk of lung cancer. *The Pharmacist's Guide to the Most Misused and Abused Drugs in America,* a compendium by pharmacist and chemistry instructor Ken Liska, states that three marijuana joints contain as much tar as twenty cigarettes, "and the practice of smoking the joint down to the end ensures that the tars get into the smoker's lungs." Liska notes that long-term heavy smoking "can cause bronchitis, irritation of the respiratory tract, and significant abnormalities in lung tissue." Others insist that the scientific evidence on this question is, as yet, inconclusive.

Claims regarding other health hazards are similarly in dispute. Some medical research evidence seemed to demonstrate, for instance, that abuse of marijuana weakens the immune system. Closer investigation indicated that the evidence could not support such a conclusion.

Opponents of marijuana use have also claimed that it causes a drop in the user's intelligence. According to Mark A. R. Kleiman, formerly of the Criminal Division of the Justice Department and now a Harvard research fellow, studies purporting to prove this "just don't hold up."

One fact about marijuana is unarguable: In contrast to heroin and cocaine, it has never been cited as a direct cause of death. There has never been a recorded instance of a fatal marijuana overdose. The drug may have caused death indirectly—for example, through auto accidents. There is no argument about the fact that pot smoking does impair driving ability in somewhat the same way that alcohol does. But no reliable statistics have ever been compiled.

One of the most widely accepted notions about pot is that it is the "gateway" drug. This is the idea that most or all of the young people who first experience drugs in the relatively mild form of a "joint" somehow feel compelled eventually to seek a stronger high. They then go on to use hard drugs like heroin, cocaine, or crack.

A National Institute on Drug Abuse study points out that young people generally abuse alcohol before they try pot. Many have also tried codeine, cough syrup, and/or glue sniffing before experimenting with heroin or cocaine. Of those who have used both alcohol and pot by their late teens or early twenties, only half graduate to hard drugs.

Few early teens try pot the first time it is offered. They are more likely to hesitate the first few times and yield to the temptation only after repeated exposure to it and under persistent pressure from their peers.

Dr. Lester Grinspoon, professor of psychiatry at the Harvard Medical School, is one of those who disagree with the gateway view of pot. He calls it "the long-discredited 'stepping-stone' hypothesis." Grinspoon points out that there is nothing in the chemical composition of marijuana that makes the move to hard drugs inevitable. Teaching that pot smoking leads to hard drug abuse "is not education but miseducation," he says, "and it will result in mistrust."

BOOMING U.S. MARIJUANA PRODUCTION

Despite slackening demand, the supply of marijuana has increased sharply. About 8,300 tons were available in the U.S. in 1985. Four years later, at least 50 percent more was on the market.

Mexico and Colombia are the two main foreign sources for marijuana. They produce between 500 and 1,000 tons a year. Until recently they shared about 60 percent of the U.S. market.

Substantial quantities are also grown in Southeast Asia, but little of this production reaches the U.S. Marijuana is much bulkier and therefore much costlier to transport than cocaine or heroin, especially over long distances. Its bulk, plus its unmistakable aroma, also make it easier to detect and capture.

One increasingly favored way to eliminate these costs and dangers has been to grow ever-mounting quantities of marijuana in the U.S. Production began to increase markedly around 1980. American growers currently supply an estimated one-quarter to one-third of the domestic demand. Most of it is grown in seven states: California, Hawaii, Kansas, Kentucky, Louisiana, Missouri, and Tennessee.

Federal, state, and local authorities have responded to stepped-up production with intensified eradication efforts. Perhaps the largest single antipot drive has been CAMP, the Campaign Against Marijuana Planting, in northern California. It was launched in 1983. Since then thousands of raids have been conducted on pot plantations, hundreds of people have been arrested, and thousands of plants cut down. They are usually carried away in bulk by helicopters, to be weighed and then burned.

CAMP raids are conducted by teams of twelve to twenty-five trained agents and volunteers from local law-enforcement agencies. Most are planned for the peak pot-growing season, from July through October. The usual method calls for CAMP airplane pilots to fly over the terrain at about a thousand feet to spot the plantations. They are then located on maps.

If the pot is being grown on private property, search

warrants are obtained from local courts. The agents are then flown to or near the site by helicopter. They cut down the plants and make arrests. All of the participating personnel are civilians, mostly from local sheriffs' offices.

California uses a judicial process called *diversion* for people caught possessing or growing marijuana for their own use. They do not have to appear in court. Instead, the charges are waived on condition that they stay out of trouble for two years. But a bill recently proposed in the state legislature would limit diversion to growers captured with ten plants or less.

Many marijuana plantations are sited on public lands. National forests are particularly favored, because they provide natural concealment. The U.S. Forest Service reported near the end of 1989 that its crackdown had eradicated more plants than ever, yet had failed to reduce the volume of marijuana grown on its lands.

To foil the authorities, the growers have turned to advanced and innovative techniques. Indoor cultivation is favored as a way to avoid being spotted by the police helicopters. Hydroponics, the science of growing plants indoors in chemicals and gravel rather than outdoors in soil, is another widely adopted method.

Special radon lamps promote lush indoor growth. Complex self-timing and self-moving systems have been developed for watering and for systematically dripping the desired nutrients into the plants' medium of growth.

A national monthly magazine, *High Times,* brings pot growers news and advertisements concerning the latest developments in marijuana-cultivation technologies. *High Times* also features a steady flow of propaganda advocating the legalization of marijuana, sponsored by NORML (National

Organization for the Reform of the Marijuana Laws).

The Drug Enforcement Administration estimates that domestic cultivation of marijuana may be approaching 10,000 tons annually. But the DEA believes that as much as half may be destroyed each year by federal, state, and local eradication campaigns.

The market value of the crop probably amounts to nearly $20 billion. Marijuana today is America's most valuable crop.

About half the domestic marijuana is sinsemilla, the superior seedless type that also has a higher THC content than the ordinary variety. It is usually sold in bundles of twenty to fifty pounds.

Hashish is almost entirely produced abroad. Despite the ravages of its long civil war, Lebanon is the chief supplier to the U.S.

THE DREAMWORLD OF HEROIN

Heroin produces its effect on the user by depressing the central nervous system. The user experiences a sense of detachment or a dreamy state that lasts for four to six hours. Frequent or long-sustained use produces a powerful physical addiction.

Heroin abuse usually begins with inhaling ("snorting") the drug. It may proceed to "skin popping"—injecting it just under the skin. The seriously addicted addict or the user who is simply looking for a faster, stronger "rush" injects it directly into a vein ("mainlining").

Heroin addicts are easy to recognize, as they "nod off" in their private dreamworld. Their lethargy makes it more difficult for them to function in the real world than abusers of some other drugs, such as marijuana or cocaine. The only thing that stirs heroin "junkies" to action is their drive to "cop" another "fix."

Attempts to give up the drug "cold turkey" (all at once, rather than gradually) almost invariably lead to withdrawal symptoms, such as chills, nausea, vomiting, convulsions, and cramps. These symptoms, though undoubtedly unpleasant, are rarely as severe as many addicts claim. In most cases they are no worse than the aches, fever, and chills of the flu. Yet it is fear of these withdrawal "agonies" that keeps many addicts from trying to break their habit.

Most heroin abusers are inner-city ghetto dwellers, which means that they are often poor and minority members. Certain multiracial groups, such as jazz and rock musicians and others in the arts, seem to be especially susceptible to the lure of heroin. Users claim they perform better and are more spontaneous and creative while they are high, but this delusion is rarely borne out by actual performance.

Heroin has never been widely popular among the middle or upper classes of any racial or ethnic group, whether in the arts, the professions, or business.

The consensus among drug experts is that the number of heroin addicts in the U.S. has remained stable at about 500,000 since the mid-1970s.

After heroin is delivered to the U.S., it may get "stepped on," or diluted, as many as seven to ten times before it reaches the consumer. Starting out 99 percent pure in an Asian or Mexican laboratory, it may be cut with lactose, quinine, cornstarch, or almost any white powdery substance. By the time the drug is sold on the street, it is usually less than 10 percent pure. Sometimes the powder contains as little as 1 to 4 percent heroin.

The user has no way of knowing how much heroin may be contained in the dose he takes. Overdoses, including fatal ones, are frequent.

If for any reason the dealer wishes to do away with some troublesome customer, the heroin can be mixed with deadly arsenic or strychnine to deliver what is known as a "hot shot."

The extreme dilution of the drug accounts in large part for the enormous profits. In one operation, a kilo of pure morphine was sold in Italy for $12,500; after being refined into heroin and cut, the drug brought $1.7 million on the street.

Heroin is a relatively expensive drug, although the price fluctuates from time to time as a reflection of supply and demand. Recently the average price of a quarter-gram packet was about forty dollars.

Since the heroin high usually lasts no more than four to six hours, hard-core addicts require several "fixes" a day. Their constantly renewed craving commonly leads them to commit street crimes, such as assault, robbery, and burglary. Heroin addicts do not usually tend to be as violent as users of crack while under the drug's influence. They can turn to extreme violence when unable to get their fix, however, or while in the throes of withdrawal.

Congressman Charles B. Rangel, chairman of the House Select Committee on Narcotics Abuse and Control, warned in an August 1990 article in the *New York Times* that heroin use was once again ominously increasing. He blamed it on law-enforcement's "single-minded focus on cocaine." The Drug Enforcement Administration, he noted, "had found an 'explosion' of increased production" in the world's opium-growing regions.

The result has been "a tremendous increase in the purity of the cut heroin sold on the streets [of the U.S.]—often five times the level normally found." This purer heroin can easily be smoked. It is favored by addicts who had been avoiding the use of needles and their accompanying danger of AIDS.

Calling for a comprehensive new drug strategy, Rangel concluded: "If we somehow get a grip on the cocaine and crack problem but end up allowing heroin to boom out of control, what will we have accomplished? We will have exchanged one misery for another."

MUSCLING IN ON THE MAFIA

From the end of World War II to the early 1980s, the Mafia maintained rigid control over most of the heroin trade in the U.S. Then other criminal organizations gradually began to nibble away at the Mafia empire. It was also weakened by a long series of relentless federal prosecutions that put many top *mafiosi* in prison for long terms.

The Chinese triads were among the mobs that took over portions of the once mighty Mafia's market. Their heroin supplies originated almost entirely within the Golden Triangle of Myanmar (formerly Burma), Thailand, and Laos.

In February 1989, the Chinese community in New York City was astonished by the arrest of seventy-one-year-old Peter Fok-leung Woo. A venerable and respected figure in New York's Chinatown, he was accused of bringing together wholesale heroin dealers and buyers for a network that stretched from Singapore to Flushing, Queens. Federal officials said they believed Woo's vast network was controlled by the 14K Triad, one of the biggest Chinese crime organizations.

Woo pleaded guilty to the charges of conspiracy to distribute heroin and conspiracy to obtain heroin for the purpose of distributing and selling it. He has not yet been sentenced as of this writing.

THE DEADLY "DESIGNER DRUGS"

The term "designer drugs" came into use in the 1980s to describe synthetic narcotics. These are drugs formulated in secret laboratories that mimic the effects of opium, morphine, and heroin.

The idea of synthetic drugs was hardly a new one. Most prescription and over-the-counter drugs are synthetic; that is, they originate not from plants or other natural sources but are entirely formulated by licensed pharmaceutical companies in their labs.

Among illegal substances, marijuana, cocaine, and opium are examples of drugs made from plants. Hence they are not synthetics. But only opium is classified as a narcotic, because it is the kind of drug that soothes the user and induces a stuporlike state and because it is physically addictive. Marijuana and cocaine are stimulants rather than narcotics.

Illegal synthetic drugs have a long history. In recent times the first to become popular were the psychedelics of the 1960s, notably LSD. In the 1970s amphetamines ("uppers"), methamphetamine ("speed") and PCP ("angel dust") came into wide use. Then came the designer narcotics of the 1980s.

These are fabricated by black-market chemists. In their clandestine labs they slightly alter the molecular structure of some existing drug, creating a new and as yet untested narcotic. Surprisingly, the new drug is technically legal, because it has not yet been outlawed by any government agency.

The market for these drugs is wide open. Bootleg recipes for their manufacture are bought and sold. The labs for making them are easy and inexpensive to set up, and they can be dismantled and moved to new sites quickly. The profits are high.

But these synthetics carry their own built-in dilemma. Even more than with other illicit drugs, the purchaser makes his buy in total ignorance of what ingredients the drugs may contain. Nor can he know what proportion of each ingredient is present. He has to have confidence in whatever the seller tells him about the drugs or the chemist who formulated them. It is a particularly dangerous form of Russian roulette.

The qualifications of the chemists who compound the drugs vary widely. Some are well trained and educated professionals who operate in the black market only because they want to supplement their regular incomes. Some are self-taught "wizards," who may or may not have any formal training but have enough talent and knowledge to design new drugs. And finally, there are others who picked up all the chemistry they know from watching others "cook."

The synthetics are often made in such a way as to be many times more potent than the drugs they imitate. Theoretically, this should work out to the buyer's advantage, since he or she should be able to use smaller doses of the more powerful drug and still get the same effect.

But often the chemist himself is unsure of the drug's exact potency, even though this may be a matter of life and death for the user. Without this knowledge, there is no way the user can sensibly regulate the amount used. Taking too much of an unknown drug can result in a crippling or fatal overdose.

The number of dead victims of such overdoses has grown steadily since the early 1980s. At first they were almost all hard-core addicts. But more recently there have been deaths among less frequent users as well.

In a large number of cases that were not immediately fatal, the users fell victim to an illness that strikingly resembles Parkinson's disease. This affliction attacks the section of the brain containing the cells that control movement. It causes an uncontrollable trembling of the head and limbs and eventual paralysis. The patient's condition often deteriorates gradually, ending in death.

Users may not show any symptoms for months, even years. When the early symptoms appear, they are often not recognized. These may include hand tremors, loss of facial expression, and muscle stiffness.

These drugs cannot be detected by most techniques of chemical analysis. They are therefore much sought after by individuals subject to mandatory drug testing, such as parolees, prisoners, and a growing number of professional workers in sensitive jobs.

Most of the synthetic narcotics that are designed to mimic heroin are called fentanyls. They usually combine a variety of substances with two painkillers, fentanyl and meperidine. These are legally controlled substances, sold mostly under the trade names Sublimaze and Demerol. Their sale is restricted to qualified medical practitioners or prescription holders. Since the synthetics concocted from them have been manipulated in the secret labs to differ in molecular structure, their sale is permitted under the law.

The materials with which the two drugs are mixed can include lactose, sucrose, mannitol (a mild baby laxative), heroin, cocaine, quinine, or any similar substance. The active ingredient may represent as little as 1 percent of the total ingredients.

The user can never be sure he is taking the right proportion of the active ingredient. It may have a different weight than the rest of the contents and may no longer be mixed evenly—if it ever was. Or the active ingredient may have sunk to the bottom of the container.

Fentanyls are known by many street names: China White (sometimes sold deceptively as a particularly pure form of Asian heroin), synthetic H, Mexican Brown (tinted with brown dye), Persian White.

Dr. William Langston testified about designer narcotics before a U.S. Senate subcommittee in 1985:

> *[There is] a Demerol lookalike called MPPP which was uncontrolled and could be sold on the street without fear of prosecution. . . . We began seeing young addicts literally frozen overnight. . . . They looked seventy or eighty years old with Parkinson's disease.*

The *San Francisco Examiner* reported in August 1984 that a man in Menlo Park, California, was found standing beside the open door of his truck, leaning over the seat. The needle was still in his arm. He had died and frozen in place as soon as he'd "shot up," an effect not unusual with a fentanyl.

An example of a designer drug capable of achieving such dire effects is 3-methyl fentanyl. Where one gram of heroin will provide about 200 "fixes," one gram of this drug will give 50,000. It is about 3,000 times stronger than morphine and 1,000 times stronger than heroin.

Some designer drugs are so potent that the proper dose

is as little as one microgram. That is less than a single grain of salt.

There is little or no synthetic cocaine on the market. It would be prohibitively expensive and time-consuming to cook up.

THE COST OF "ECSTASY"

A new designer drug emerged in the mid-1980s. It was popularly called Ecstasy, XTC, Adam, or MDMA. Ecstasy is chemically related to methamphetamine, nutmeg, mescaline, and commonly used nasal decongestants based on pseudoephedrine. It has hallucinogenic properties, plunging the user into dreams and visions that are sometimes filled with delight, sometimes with terror.

This drug had first come out in the sixties, but most users preferred LSD because it was considerably stronger. It was then adopted for use by many psychotherapists. They found that in small doses it relaxed and opened up their patients, aiding treatment.

From a production of a mere 10,000 doses in 1976, it zoomed to about half a million by 1985. But as its use spread, hospitals and drug clinics began to receive increasing numbers of emergency cases. They featured severe anxiety reactions, depression, psychotic episodes, and some deaths.

The Drug Enforcement Administration then listed the drug on Schedule I, a classification that includes heroin, marijuana, LSD, and other illegal drugs that have a high potential for abuse and no accepted medical use. Dealing Ecstasy became a crime punishable with fifteen-year prison terms and heavy fines. Possession became a misdemeanor. The DEA went after labs in several states and shut them down.

One effect was to boost the price from a hundred dollars a gram to three hundred dollars.

At the core of this complex story lies a troubling question: With so many grave dangers awaiting the unwary user, what factors have caused so many Americans to become trapped, putting their very lives at risk?

7

The Causes of Drug Abuse

Addiction has been defined in various ways. Most experts see it as a dependence on a drug that may be physical or psychological or both. It is a progressive disease; that is, it keeps getting worse. If drug abuse is continued for long periods, it eventually undermines the addict's health. Untreated, it can be fatal.

IS THERE AN ADDICTIVE PERSONALITY?

Addiction is a lifelong, chronic disease. No one is ever fully and finally "cured." An addict may conquer the habit and stop taking drugs, but he must always consider himself only a "recovering" addict. He will always have to actively resist the powerful temptation to relapse. The most widely recommended way to stay "clean" is to regularly attend meetings of some self-help group like Narcotics Anonymous or Cocaine Anonymous.

Other countries, too, have their drug addicts, their users and abusers. None has as high a proportion as the U.S. Why is this so? There is no simple answer, but many theories.

The most fundamental fact about drugs is that they give pleasure or at least ease pain and stress—for a while. And the U.S. has the world's highest proportion of people who can afford to pay for pleasure. Sheer affluence enables many at the upper end of the economic scale to seek pleasure and escape life's problems through drugs and drinking.

In the 1970s and through the mid-1980s it was fashionable in well-to-do circles to use cocaine. It was a social drug, fun to use at parties and in bars, clubs, and discos. Many believed the drug was not harmful. But as recreational use turned to addiction for many, as the crack epidemic spread, and as public opinion became increasingly hostile to drug abuse, the affluent cut down on their involvement with drugs.

The situation is drastically different at the opposite end of the socioeconomic scale. In the inner-city ghettos, our most impoverished citizens live lives close to hopelessness and despair. Drugs and alcohol are all too easily available ways to forget one's troubles. Drug use here shows little sign of declining.

Another view of the causes of drug abuse lays most of the blame on the psychological makeup of drug abusers. A version that was influential for many years was the theory of the addictive or addiction-prone personality. Advocates for this view held that addiction could be predicted in individuals with a certain combination of personal traits.

According to this view, the most likely candidates for

addiction are emotionally unstable, immature, self-centered, and require instant satisfaction. They are unable to cope with stress of any kind or develop deep feelings toward others. They are habitual liars, and they try constantly to manipulate others. Drugs give them not only relief and escape from their troubles but also an exaggerated sense of confidence and power.

The trouble with this theory is that addicts vary tremendously. People of every psychological type have proven susceptible to drugs or alcohol. There is no such person as a typical addict. Studies of individuals raised in the same families show that they often have completely different personalities. One may become an addict; a brother or sister may never touch illegal drugs.

A research project at the Harvard Medical School followed a group of men from adolescence through their midforties. Some of them became alcoholics, though their personalities were no different from the rest. The alcoholics did eventually fall victim to a variety of psychological problems, but these were caused by the alcoholism—not the other way around.

The addict's tendency to lie and manipulate others also turns out in most cases to be a result, rather than a cause, of addiction. Once gripped by the desperate drug craving, they have to lie and "hustle" people all the time to get money for their habit.

In the words of John Grabowski, a researcher at the University of Texas Health Science Center in Houston,

To me, the notion of an addictive personality is conceptually just not very useful. It presumes all sorts of things about prediction I don't think we are capable of doing.

Most psychologists and drug counselors today agree that personality is an important factor, but they add that a whole complex of other interacting forces must be considered. These include the addict's family and friends, education, socioeconomic status and job prospects, even biochemical makeup and biological reaction to drugs.

Some individuals undoubtedly turn to drugs out of a deep need to mask mental distress. But success or failure in dealing with stress is not usually enough to turn an otherwise normal person into an addict. It is the drug and its biochemical effects on mind and body that create the chemical dependency known as addiction.

THE VARIETIES OF STRESS

The historical context in which an addiction occurs can be another determining factor. In the 1960s, use of LSD and other hallucinogenics was an approved form of rebellion among the young. The popular slogan of the times was "Turn on, tune in, drop out." These "mind-expanding" drugs went out of favor in the seventies and still have only limited appeal.

The Vietnam War provides another historical context. Combat soldiers in that conflict experienced extraordinary stress. About a third of those between the ages of seventeen and twenty-three used heroin or some other form of opium. Half of the using group indulged regularly. Yet this was an average group of Americans, no different psychologically from others.

The drugs were easy to get, they were high quality, and they were cheap. The soldiers did not have to do business with high-priced dealers or other criminal elements. Nor did they face the problem of dirty, contaminated needles, since most of them merely snorted the heroin.

Follow-up research showed that less than 10 percent used it after returning home. Of those who had become addicted in Vietnam, less than 2 percent persisted in their habit in the U.S.

Studies suggest that there are links between the intensity of a soldier's combat experience, his suffering from Post-traumatic Stress Disorder, and his drug addiction. Post-traumatic Stress Disorder, or PTSD, is a mental disturbance that afflicts some soldiers who have had shocking or terrifying experiences ("traumas") in battle.

Many of these soldiers resort to alcohol or drugs in order to relieve the intense mental and emotional pain aroused when memories of such experiences emerge into their conscious minds. The more severe the PTSD, the more severe the addiction. The studies indicate that stopping drug abuse would have been easier for those Vietnam veterans who had little or no combat experience.

As was the case in Vietnam, the sheer availability of drugs has a lot to do with the amount of abuse in any given locale. The presence of crack on street corners in so many neighborhoods makes it that much harder to resist.

An estimated 40 percent of all addicts may have suffered from mental or emotional disorders that led them to drugs. New research findings indicate that many of these addicts may have inherited certain chemical abnormalities in the brain. These genetic factors may be the underlying reason why many such individuals become addicted more quickly than others and are much harder to cure. Insufficient quantities of certain chemicals in the brain—or, in some cases, an excess of the same chemicals—can lead to depression, anxiety, or extreme restlessness. People suffering from such genetic imbalances use drugs as a kind of self-medication to restore a proper chemical balance within the brain.

This research may eventually lead to the development of new strategies for treating large numbers of addicts. Early detection of those who are most vulnerable to a specific addiction may soon become possible. Then medications specifically aimed at correcting their chemical imbalances could be prescribed.

Depressed individuals often discover to their sorrow that the lift they get from a drug like cocaine is a short-term benefit. The longer they take the drug, the more they have to take to get the same lift. Too often they find that after a time the drug actually depresses them further.

Many cocaine users say the drug only enhances whatever mood they are in. If they are having a great time at a party, the drug will heighten the enjoyment. People who are already depressed or who find themselves in a depressing environment find that the drug often lowers them to the depths of despair.

Some addicts start using drugs because they are shy, and they hope it will loosen them up so that they can communicate better with others. And at first, some drugs may do that. But long-term use has the opposite effect. People frequently high on marijuana, for instance, become too self-absorbed and lethargic to relate well to others.

Religious and ethnic factors, too, play a role. For example, Irish Americans and Native Americans have high rates of alcoholism. Asian and Jewish Americans have low rates. Low rates are associated with such customs as drinking with people of the opposite sex, or with people of other generations, or with meals, or as part of a religious ceremony linked to a holiday celebration. Many who rarely drink belong to a religious or ethnic group that considers drunkenness shameful. Drug abuse is almost certainly subject to similar influences.

One theory asserts that occasional or recreational use of drugs invariably leads to addiction. But the limited available evidence indicates that probably fewer than 10 percent of the millions who use cocaine do so every day. For other drugs, the ratio of addicts to recreational or occasional users rarely exceeds 15 percent.

YOUNGSTERS' YEARNINGS

The teenage years are a time of great vulnerability. Adolescents are filled with curiosity, eager for risk and excitement, rebellious yet impatient to be accepted as grown-up. They worry about the tumultuous mental, emotional, and bodily changes that puberty brings. They worry about dating, athletic competition, college and career choices, ambivalent feelings about separation from their parents. Above all, they yearn to be popular among their peers.

When they first experiment with drugs, the young most commonly start with alcohol and then, usually under pressure from friends, try marijuana. At first they are likely to use it only moderately, for recreational purposes. But for some, occasional use soon deteriorates into abuse, and they too often get into hard drugs.

As youngsters' drug involvement deepens, their behavior changes. They begin to avoid their straight friends, who now seem less interesting or even cause the drug-using teen to feel guilty. They seek out other users, often older than they.

At home, their moods shift chaotically. They become uncooperative and withdrawn. Normally happy-go-lucky youths turn sad, depressed, isolated. Thoughts of suicide rise up as never before to haunt them. The actual suicide rate for adolescents has tripled since the 1960s, though the exact proportion linked to drug abuse is unknown.

The family may be at the root of the problem. Often the families of youngsters having difficulty are in disorder, unable to care or do anything to help. Communication may have broken down among its members. Mutual respect, not to mention love, may have been eroded into indifference or active hostility. The parents may have alienated the kids by attempting to overcontrol them, or by not controlling them enough.

A very high proportion of drug-using youngsters live in broken homes headed by a single parent, usually the mother. In such situations, normal discipline may be weakened. The child who resents the absence of the father often becomes contemptuous of all forms of authority. He may seek role models outside the home.

In many cases, children turn to drugs because their parents are poor role models, especially if the parents use alcohol or drugs. Even parents who habitually use legal drugs like Valium or other tranquilizers may unwittingly be leading their offspring toward drug abuse.

This is a particular problem with the former "flower children" of the 1960s. They went through their adolescence and early twenties at a time when taking drugs was an accepted pattern among the young. Now they are having children of their own. Many continue to use drugs while raising their kids. Inevitably, the kids imitate their elders.

Pro-drug messages in varied forms assault the young

from many directions. The entertainment media often portray drug use as glamorous or amusing. Certain rock stars and their music convey similar messages.

A drug habit usually costs more than the average teen can afford. Once the allowance is used up, plus the possible wages from some part-time job if the kid is still capable of holding a job, he may begin to deal drugs or steal. Girls may turn to prostitution; less often, boys may do so, too.

And all the while, the craving keeps getting more urgent. The high that felt so wonderful at the start is now harder and harder to reach.

Chronic drug abusers often get themselves expelled from school, and possibly from home as well. Holding a job becomes impossible. They adopt criminal activity as a way of life. Sooner or later, there is trouble with the law. The youngster hits bottom.

At this stage, there remain only two choices. The teen must accept treatment, carry out its requirements conscientiously, and stick with it till he is judged drug-free and released. That way lies hope. Or he can stick with his addiction and the criminal behavior it entails. That way lies tragedy.

WOMEN'S STRESSES

Young single women are subject to special pressures. In the modern world they are urged to do well academically and go to college, but at the same time they are pressured to be popular, attractive, part of the "in" group. When they tell doctors about physical ailments that may result from these tensions, the doctors tend to prescribe tranquilizers much more frequently than they do for male patients. The door is opened to young women's perception of drugs as an approved way of easing stress.

One result is that twice as many women use depressants (barbiturates and other kinds of sleeping pills, as well as tranquilizers) as men do.

Women today are entering many career fields formerly open only to men. As they try to find their way amid these new circumstances, balancing their personal lives with their careers, they experience new forms of stress. On the one hand they are expected to be sweet and attractive and feminine; on the other they have to master the arts of aggression and self-advancement in a competitive world.

Diet-conscious women often turn to amphetamines (like Benzedrine, Dexedrine, or Dexamyl) as aids to weight loss. Men use these drugs, too, but in much smaller numbers. Users find that they rapidly develop a tolerance for the drug and need to increase the dosage. Any weight loss due to the drug often proves to be temporary and short-term, usually lasting only two to four weeks. Attempts to lose more through increased use of the drug can have dangerous side effects, sometimes leading to extreme mental disturbance.

In the public mind, serious drug use is invariably and inevitably a cause of criminal activity. A discussion of the drugs-crime linkage will show that the problem is more complex than is generally believed.

8

The Much-Disputed Link: Drugs and Crime

One of the most often heard statements about the drug epidemic is the seemingly obvious generalization that drug abuse causes crime. In this view, the single most important factor responsible for the alarming rise in the level of crime in the U.S. is the unceasing quest of drug abusers for money to feed their habits. The rising incidence of violent crimes in particular is said to be due to the influence of drugs like crack, which are commonly believed to turn their users toward violence.

WHICH IS THE CAUSE, WHICH IS THE EFFECT?

The National Institute on Drug Abuse has established a Drug Use Forecasting System to gather statistics on this question. Males arrested on criminal charges in twenty major cities were tested for drug use. Between 50 and 85 percent tested positive for one or more drugs. Do these figures prove that drug use is a direct cause of crime?

In 1979, only 25 percent of convicted criminals admitted committing their crimes while under a drug's influence. By 1986 the proportion had risen to 35 percent. Is there a link between these figures and rising crime rates?

But before conclusions can be drawn, other facts must be considered. Drug testing of arrestees did not begin until very recently. The lack of previous statistics means there is no reliable historical basis for comparing today's figures with past crime rates. The new test figures can be interpreted as showing only that the rising percentages of arrestees testing positive for cocaine may reflect the rising popularity of crack. The figures may also demonstrate that high percentages of criminals use drugs—or, putting it differently, that criminal behavior and drug abuse go together. This long-known fact scarcely constitutes a new discovery.

Such survey findings do not necessarily prove that drug abusers commit crimes *because* they use drugs. The types of individuals most likely to use drugs come from the kinds of backgrounds that produce the highest numbers of criminals. Criminals and drug users often share low education, broken families, and low social status. Drug abuse is a normal and accepted part of a career criminal's life-style.

However, criminals who use drugs do undoubtedly commit more crimes than nonusing criminals. Though their drug use may not force them into crime, it does intensify their criminal behavior.

The common perception is that people develop a drug habit first and then steal to maintain it. Yet a survey of inmates of state prisons showed that less than one-seventh had ever used a major addicting drug, such as heroin or cocaine, before their first arrest. Usually they had abused alcohol, marijuana, pep pills, and other "soft" drugs, which are associated with considerably lower crime rates.

Surveys of women had similar results. Most had started on their criminal careers before they ever got into hard drugs. In his 1984 book *The War on Drugs,* criminologist James A. Inciardi quoted a twenty-two-year-old prostitute he had interviewed:

> *"I've often thought that if I'd never started with the drugs I'd never have ended up turning tricks [working as a prostitute] every day. But the more you make me think about it, the more I think that one had nothing to do with the other. You grow up in a place where everything is a real mess. Your father's a thief, your mother's a whore, your kid sister gets herself some new clothes by [being intimate with] the landlord's son, your brother's in [prison], your boy friend got shot trying to pull down [rob] a store, and everybody else around you is either smokin' dope, shooting stuff, taking pills, stealing with both hands, or workin' on their backs, or all of the above. . . .*
>
> *"I can't really say why I started stealing, using [heroin], and walking the streets. It was all around me and it was an easy way out. . . . "*

The National Institute of Justice did studies of the prisoners in three states in the mid-1980s. It found that a majority had a history of heroin abuse. Drug abusers in general were shown to be likely perpetrators of violent crimes.

About 25 percent of all homicides in several cities were found to be drug-related in these studies. They also showed that an astonishing 3 percent of all young criminals were responsible for 75 percent of all robberies and half of all felony assaults. All were pill, cocaine, or heroin abusers. Robberies and assaults were found to be rare among nondrug abusers.

Inciardi has classified drug-related violent crimes into three categories:

- Psychopharmacological violence, the type that is brought on by the effects of the drugs on the users;

- Economically compulsive violence, the type brought on by the need for money to support the drug habit;

- Systemic violence, the type brought on by conflicts within the drug world, such as: competition for control of markets; enforcement of tacitly agreed-upon rules; robberies of dealers or retaliation for such robberies; or punishment for selling bad dope, for failures to pay debts, or for many other transgressions.

Of course, many violent crimes have no relation at all to drugs. But crimes that are drug-related seem to follow certain patterns.

HOW DRUG USE INTENSIFIES CRIME

A Baltimore study corroborated the conclusion that a relatively small number of criminal drug abusers is responsible for a large part of all crimes. It focused on a multiracial group of 354 male heroin users. Over a period of 9.5 years, this group committed an almost unbelievable total of about 750,000 crimes. Some criminologists estimate that the nation's entire population of addicts commits as many as 100 million crimes a year.

During periods when these addicts were in the grip of their habit, they committed crimes on 255 days of the year. When they were drug-free, that number dropped to only 65.

Since 1965, several nationwide studies have gathered evidence as to whether drug abuse truly causes crime or merely stimulates already existing criminal careers. First there was President Lyndon Johnson's Commission on Law Enforcement and Administration of Justice. In 1975 the National Institute on Drug Abuse (NIDA) held a one-day workshop, bringing together the nation's leading experts on this problem. Both concluded that a direct causal link could not be proven.

NIDA also sponsored an extensive study that ran from 1977 to 1985. Over 3,000 hard-drug users were interviewed, mostly in Dade County, Florida. On average, they had begun using alcohol at the age of 13.7, marijuana at 15, sedatives at 17.1, heroin at 18.9, cocaine at 19.4. These were heavy users, some indulging in as many as five drugs.

Virtually all had committed crimes. The median age at which they started was 15, well before they were hooked on hard drugs. But these early actions were of the type generally classified as juvenile delinquency, rarely involving major crimes. Only later, after getting hooked on the hard stuff, had they gone on to active adult criminal careers.

Gender seems to make little difference in the operation of this pattern of behavior. In a New York study, 78 percent of 261 male suspects who submitted to voluntary urinalysis between October and December 1988 were found to have traces of drugs in their systems; 76 percent of 103 women did.

The only difference related to prostitution. More drug-using girls than boys tended to get into that way of life. Most were addicted to hard drugs when they did so. But they had usually been engaged in criminal activity before falling into addiction.

Statistical studies of criminal behavior such as those described above cannot claim total accuracy. They are based on arrest records. This is an inherently biased source, for only a tiny percentage of all crimes—less than half of 1 percent—leads to arrests. For obvious reasons, studies of criminals who have not been caught and arrested are not feasible.

DRUGS AND MIDDLE-CLASS CRIME

The spread of cocaine and crack use among the middle class has led to increased crime rates among this group as well. But middle-class crimes differ from those most commonly committed by less affluent drug abusers. Middle-class crimes are almost entirely white-collar, nonviolent acts such as fraud or embezzlement. Theft, robbery, and burglary are the most common crimes committed by drug abusers from the less advantaged classes, with far higher levels of violence.

Living amid street cultures that are simultaneously drug-ridden and crime-infested can produce unpredictable criminal behavior even among youngsters who do not use drugs and have previously committed no crimes. A notorious example is the April 1989 rape and near-fatal beating of a woman jogger in

New York's Central Park by a pack of East Harlem teenagers.

Considering the nature of this particular group of adolescents, the sheer wantonness and brutality of the crime seemed to make no sense. Almost all belonged to fairly prosperous, law-abiding, conscientious families. Few had any police records. Most were good students. But their neighborhood was rife with lawlessness.

The power balance in neighborhoods like this one had shifted from adults to the young because of the street drug trade. Many teens living in such areas sell crack to adults—sometimes even their own parents. Some give their parents a share of their drug profits to help support the family. The authority of parents accepting drug money from their children is inevitably weakened in such an abnormal situation.

Extreme violence has been common in such neighborhoods ever since the rise of crack. Violent local teenage gangs are ruled by out-of-control leaders. Sociological studies have shown, surprisingly, that gang leaders often come from stable families.

Sociologists who have lived in and studied East Harlem and similar neighborhoods all over the country say that, to be respected in the community, young men have to prove they can be brutal in order to avoid being picked on. For drug-free youngsters as for those who use, their role models are drawn from the savage drug world they see around them.

Drug abuse and criminal behavior are both infecting ever younger individuals. "Drug use," said Hunter Hurst, director of the National Center for Juvenile Justice, "used to be a decision of adolescence; now it's a fourth-grade decision."

Referrals to the juvenile courts of thirteen-, fourteen-, and fifteen-year-olds accused of serious crimes have risen steeply and steadily since the late 1970s.

"CRACK DOWN ON THEM!"

Public opinion about criminal justice policies for drug-related crime is inflamed by rising crime rates and related developments such as the invasion of neighborhoods by crack houses.

Addicts have a nickname for these: "7-24 houses." They are open seven days a week, twenty-four hours a day.

Crack houses are usually rundown and a neighborhood eyesore. Disputes are common, often accompanied by screaming, shouting, and all too often by stabbings and shootings. Prostitutes impatient for their next crack "hit" often solicit openly on residential streets near crack houses. Neighborhoods close to crack houses often have more burglaries and robberies than do other areas because addicts do not like to stray too far from their drug supply.

The natural reactions of the public and of politicians to these outward signs of drug crime have been anger and a determination to crack down hard. Experience has shown, however, that policies that are too punitive do not work. In 1973, New York State passed a set of antidrug laws that were the toughest in the country. They provided, for instance, for mandatory life sentences for drug dealers (New York has no death sentence).

It soon became apparent that juries were reluctant to convict young dealers when it meant sending them to prison for the rest of their lives. In some cases, usually where no crime of violence had been committed, the juries proved reluctant even to convict adults because of the long sentences mandated by the new laws. The mandatory life provision had to be repealed.

Some of the tough drug laws passed in many states in

the 1980s provide not only for longer sentences for drug offenders but also specify the sentences judges must impose. Previously, judges had considerable leeway in choosing the exact sentence for a particular crime. For example, if the law allowed for a sentence ranging from five to fifteen years, the judge could set the actual term to be served anywhere within those limits. Today's harsher sentences tend to allow for much narrower ranges or none at all, giving judges little or no choice.

Under the older system, criminals were often willing to "plea bargain." They would plead guilty if prosecutors and judges agreed to reduce the charges and the sentence. This system eliminated the need for many trials. It lightened the load in our already overcrowded courts and saved prosecutors and judges considerable time and the states considerable money.

But under the new system, offenders know they are likely to get just about the same mandatory sentence whether they plead guilty or force the state to go through a trial. Having nothing to gain or lose, they insist on a trial. The result has been an intolerable logjam in the courts.

One theory underlying the enthusiasm for harsh punishment of drug offenders is that the threat of severe penalties will deter potential drug abusers from becoming involved in the drug scene. Harsh punishments will therefore prevent a significant proportion of crime. There is some evidence that such threats do have some effect on the middle and upper classes. But there are no reliable statistics that they deter the economically deprived drug abusers who make up the vast majority of the group.

The contention that drug abuse causes crime is at best a partial explanation and, in important ways, a misleading one.

It ignores the fact that criminal behavior most typically precedes abuse of hard drugs. And it fails to consider the complex social, economic, and psychological factors that lie at the root of crime. Formulation of effective strategies for dealing with the problems of drug abuse and crime requires an unemotional, unbiased, in-depth understanding of the true causal relationships.

A crucial question is whether drug abuse should be considered primarily a criminal problem, best solved by strict law enforcement and punishment, or a medical one, best approached with an emphasis on treatment.

9

Many Roads to Treatment

The National Institute on Drug Abuse estimates that as of the late 1980s, there were about 4 million drug addicts in the U.S. Addicts or serious drug users are defined as persons who use one or more drugs at least 200 times in a twelve-month period.

Not all of these people need or want treatment to rid them of their habit. In a September 1989 report to the nation on his plans for warring against the drug menace, President Bush estimated that 25 percent of the addicts could stop abusing drugs with no treatment other than the care and support of their family, friends, and clergy. Another 25 percent were hard-core users who either did not wish to stop or could not. That left half of all addicts—about 2 million individuals—who might benefit from well-designed professional treatment programs.

THE "TREATMENT ON DEMAND"
CONTROVERSY

But the existing treatment facilities are not nearly adequate
to cope with such large numbers. According to NIDA statistics for 1987, the latest figures available, fewer than 350,000
patients can be accommodated at any one time in the 5,000
treatment centers currently operating. Counting those who
complete their treatment and leave during any given year,
those who drop out, and repeaters, about 800,000 addicts can
be treated annually. More than a million are left out of the
system, wanting treatment but unable to get it.

Yet drug treatment has mushroomed into one of the
fastest-growing businesses in the country. By 1990, private
rehab centers had attained a total yearly income estimated at
$1 billion a year. As new federal, state, and local programs
come into operation, the treatment industry will undoubtedly
expand enormously.

Nondrug users are sometimes surprised at the notion
that so many addicts yearn to be cured. Some view addicts
as devoting their lives to a ceaseless quest for self-indulgent,
drug-generated pleasure or escape from reality.

Actually, most addicts' lives are far from happy. For one
thing, the longer an addict has been on drugs, the harder it
is to get that blissful high experienced at the beginning. Long-
time addicts have to take more of the drug to approach the
original high. Second, the addict's life during the hours between highs is usually dogged by the constantly renewed
need to get money for the drug, and then by the desperate
urge to "cop" from a "connection." Third, the drugs have
usually impaired the addict's mental and physical health seriously enough to cause a variety of discomforts and sufferings.

Antidrug officials in the major cities are beset by concentrations of large numbers of addicts. They are urging the fastest and widest possible expansion of treatment facilities. But federal officials point out that there is no agreement on the most effective modes of treatment. They argue that expansion should be carried out gradually while treatments are thoroughly evaluated.

"There's a fire going on right now," said Dr. Robert G. Newman, president of New York's Beth Israel Medical Center, site of the country's largest methadone treatment center for heroin addicts. That fire, he says, is

killing people and our communities. Sure, I agree we need evaluation, but what are we going to do with hundreds of thousands of people who need help this minute?

Other experts admit the urgency of the problem but suggest that the number of treatment slots can be increased at the same time as modes of treatment are studied and improved.

Federal, state, and local authorities all plan substantially increased expenditures for drug treatment in the 1990s. But no detailed national plans exist on how the money should be spent or how to evaluate the results.

Many politicians and drug authorities assert that the goal should be "treatment on demand." Under this plan, a surplus of treatment or rehabilitation slots would be created so that no addict seeking treatment would ever be turned away. As things stand, thousands of addicts can only get their names on long waiting lists at overcrowded centers. Then they have to wait weeks or months before being admitted. Many become discouraged and stop seeking the professional help they so desperately need. Some centers are so full that they no longer bother even to maintain waiting lists.

Desperation sometimes drives addicts to extreme measures. Alexis Vega, a thirty-four-year-old crack addict from the South Bronx, had applied to a variety of programs, only to be told he would have to wait. Even when he got himself arrested and pleaded in court to be placed in treatment, he got no help. Finally he smashed some windows at a police station to force yet another arrest. This time he was brought before Criminal Court Judge John Moore, who was sympathetic. Moore made a phone call and at long last got Vega enrolled at a treatment center.

Even sadder was the case of Joletha Simmons. The thirty-four-year-old addict allowed a *Washington Post* photographer to take pictures as she prepared and injected heroin. The photos even showed how she puffed up her cheeks to make a vein in her neck stand out before plunging the needle in. They were published in a Sunday edition of the *Post.* "She is desperate to kick her habit," the newspaper explained, "and hopes that the publicity will help her get into a drug treatment program." Ms. Simmons did eventually get enrolled.

A number of authorities question the need for treatment on demand. Dr. Bob Gilhooly, director of substance abuse technical services at Roanoke Valley Mental Health Service in Virginia, says he is "suspicious of 'walk-ins.' " These are addicts who come to treatment centers on their own, without referrals from doctors, hospitals, or courts. "They're just looking to get 'detoxed' [get their bodies cleared of drugs] for a couple of days and go back out." Gilhooly feels such addicts are uninterested in serious, prolonged treatment and have not yet made the tough decision to break their drug habit permanently.

Others question the reliability of waiting lists. Many addicts get on several lists but then do not wait for admission. Their motivation to get treatment doesn't last long enough to ensure that they show up when space becomes available.

Bush administration officials believe that creation of sufficient facilities to provide treatment on demand would be impossibly inefficient and expensive. It was, however, included as one of the ultimate objectives of the AntiDrug Abuse Act of 1989.

THE DROPOUT PROBLEM

The statistics on addicts staying long enough to complete their treatment are discouraging. On average, less than half stick it out to the end.

Most residential facilities, for example, where addict-patients live while they work out their problems, require their patients to remain for at least eighteen months to two years. The average patient leaves after only eleven months.

Another problem is that treatment slots that become available often do not match the needs of local addicts. Most of the available slots are in centers that were set up at a time when heroin addiction constituted the main problem, and they are designed primarily to treat that type of addiction. Today heroin junkies are far outnumbered by cocaine addicts.

Cocaine addicts are more likely than heroin junkies to be using other drugs at the same time. Their treatment needs to be quite different. One result of the failure to coordinate treatments with addict needs is that some centers have empty beds, while others have long waiting lists.

A solution to this problem would be improved referral services. An example is the Assessment and Referral Center in Kansas City, Missouri. It receives about a thousand calls a month from addicts seeking help. The center diagnoses the addicts and then refers them to facilities that match their needs.

To deal with the problems of addicts who avoid treatment or drop out, a legal technique called civil commitment has been adopted in nineteen states. Here the choice is no longer left to the addict. Parents, as one example, may obtain civil commitment orders from courts to commit drug-abusing children for mandatory treatment. In some cases friends or relatives may apply for civil commitment for adults as well as children.

In other states, it is illegal to compel anyone to undergo treatment unless that person has been convicted of a crime. Courts can mandate treatment as part of a convicted person's punishment. Enforcement of treatment orders is known to be lax in prisons, however. Success rates are low, and recidivism rates (the number of abusers who go back on drugs after treatment) are high.

Some authorities believe that the "shock" effect of being compelled to accept treatment has a positive effect on addicts' attitudes. Others disagree, arguing that treatment is rarely effective unless the addict has been self-motivated enough to make a voluntary choice.

New York State has the largest number of addicts. According to a report released in 1990 by the National Association of State Alcohol and Drug Abuse Directors, there were more than 800,000 drug abusers in New York in need of treatment in 1989. Not surprisingly, this state leads the nation in both public and private funding for drug-abuse treatment. Yet it could accommodate only 93,000 people in treatment programs in 1989, the report estimated. Some 5,000 were on waiting lists, and the average wait for an outpatient slot was sixty-five days.

MODES OF TREATMENT

The first problem is to get patients into treatment. Usually they agree to it only when confronted with some sort of crisis. They may be having medical or financial trouble. They may be unable to get or hold a job. They may be in difficulty with the law. The problem may be interpersonal, like an inability to get along with a spouse, family, or friends. Or it may be psychological, stemming from an addict's depression, paranoia, hallucinations, or delusions.

Some addicts adopt a pose known as "denial." They insist that they could stop taking drugs any time they want to and deny that they are, in fact, hooked. These addicts are so resistant to treatment that some therapists refuse them as patients.

Despite the problems associated with treatment programs, their benefits have been proven in several long-term studies. One of these was the Treatment Outcome Prospective Study (TOPS), which was supported by the National Institute on Drug Abuse and published in October 1989. The TOPS study examined 10,000 individuals admitted to treatment in ten cities across the country beginning in 1979, 1980, and 1981. Its findings included the following:

- Three to five years after treatment, less than 20 percent of clients in any type of treatment program were regular users of any drug, except marijuana.

- For all drugs except marijuana, about 40 to 50 percent of users stopped, and 70 to 80 percent cut down on drug use. For marijuana, about 20 percent stopped and 40 percent cut down.

- The proportion of clients involved in predatory crimes such as robbery and assault was one-third to one-half of pretreatment levels in all types of treatment programs when examined three to five years after treatment.

- All types of programs studied resulted in gains in the percentage of clients employed full time after treatment.

Another NIDA-supported study, the Drug Abuse Report Program, examined 44,000 individuals admitted to treatment between 1969 and 1974. Its impressive findings included these statistics:

- Daily opiate use declined significantly in all types of treatment from nearly 100 percent to approximately 25 percent in the third year after discharge.

- Arrest rates decreased by 74 percent after treatment for all DARP clients.

- Employment rose from 33 percent before admission to 57 percent in the year after discharge for all DARP clients.

In addition, the NIDA reviewed a number of studies, including TOPS and DARP, in 1988 and concluded, among other findings, that drug-abuse treatment significantly reduces the transmission of AIDS among intravenous drug users. The lowest rates of infection are found among persons in treatment the longest.

What modes of treatment are available?

Crisis Intervention.

Ed Storti is a specialist who has developed techniques for convincing addicts to go into treatment. The first step, he writes in his book *Crisis Intervention,* is for a relative or someone else on close terms with the addict to call a crisis intervention center for help. Interventionists may also be available at hospitals, treatment centers, and schools. Some marriage and family therapists have been trained in this method.

The interventionist will then meet, perhaps several times, with those most closely involved, though not yet with the addict. He or she may also refer the relatives to Alanon (the national association for relatives and friends of alcoholics and drug abusers) or some similar group.

One of the specialist's tasks is to persuade the relatives that they will have to change as the patient begins to recover. This can be more difficult than it sounds. In a high proportion of cases, people close to addicts "enable" them to persist in their addictions. They may supply the money, or excuse the addictive behavior and tolerate it, or simply pretend it is not happening or is not serious. They have to face up to their own actions, however disguised these may be as good intentions.

When the group has been melded into an effective team, the addict is called in. At this meeting the specialist plays the dominant role. Storti has found that most addicts want help, but they respond best to someone they are not emotionally involved with. The specialist explains the urgency of the need for treatment. All the while he expresses concern and respect for the addict and gets the others to do the same. Most addicts accept the idea of treatment at this stage.

If the addict still refuses, some sort of specific warning

may help. His spouse may declare her intention of leaving, or his employer may threaten to fire him, or some other form of leverage may be applied.

When and if the addict is finally persuaded, the interventionist and others in the team accompany the addict to the treatment center. Care is taken to make sure he is properly enrolled and well started.

Individual Therapy.

This kind of treatment consists mainly of intensive one-on-one sessions with a trained therapist, often a psychologist or psychiatrist. The therapist helps the patient to plumb his own background and the often hidden motives underlying his behavior. By making the patient aware of his real motives and helping him to face them honestly, the therapist opens the patient to the possibility of change.

One of the most difficult tasks facing the therapist is persuading patients to strip away the complex web of lies and self-deceptions they have been hiding behind. One patient told San Francisco therapist Joanne Baum, "I was telling so many lies all the time that even when I *could* tell the truth, I made something up."

At the carefully chosen right stage of treatment, the therapist will bring in the family. They must be helped to understand the true nature of the addict's problem and must learn to be supportive.

Most therapists will also arrange for the patient to participate in group sessions. Here the patient can air any problems and get feedback and suggestions from other patients. The group is both supportive and confrontational at the same time.

Individual therapy is a relatively expensive type of treatment favored by the well-to-do. It is generally beyond the reach of the mass of addicts.

Outpatient Therapy.

In this form of treatment, patients continue to live at home and work at their jobs, if they have any. They are required only to visit a clinic for treatment several times a week. It is much less expensive than individual therapy, both in time and money. It causes the least disruption in the patients' lives and in those of persons close to them.

Outpatient treatment can include individual or group psychotherapy. In the former, the patient discusses the problem with a counselor or therapist on a one-to-one basis. Group therapy brings together a small number of patients, often with a similar problem. They meet under the guidance of a therapist—sometimes a former addict who has received special training.

In the group, patients are encouraged to share their innermost thoughts and feelings. Any who try to conceal or mask their true selves, or who justify their addictive behavior, may find themselves abruptly brought to order by the other patients. As addicts themselves, they know all the deceptions and self-deceptions.

The patient's spouse or other relatives may also be invited to discuss the problem with the therapists. Often joint sessions with the addict are arranged, in which the relatives confront the addict with the damage the addiction has done to all of them.

Outpatient therapy has the disadvantage that it does not remove the addict from the often unhealthy environment that fostered the addiction. Above all, it does not separate the patient from drug sources. It works best with highly motivated patients. They will usually be encouraged to attend meetings of Alcoholics Anonymous, Narcotics Anonymous, or some similar self-help group.

Inpatient Therapy.

The most usual forms of inpatient treatment are hospitalization or commitment to some type of residential rehabilitation center. These are recommended if the patient is doing or threatening to do serious self-harm or harm to others, if he is taking extremely poor care of himself, if he is risking grave danger in order to get drugs, if his social contacts are detrimental to his welfare, if he has severe medical or psychological complications, or if he is unwilling or unable to carry through with an outpatient program.

In a controlled setting of this type, the patient can be kept drug-free while getting a thorough evaluation. Trained personnel can determine the extent to which the patient's drug use stems from multiple problems. These might include parental drug use, or physical or sexual abuse. The patient may be having serious school or job problems, or may be in trouble with the law. He or she may be experiencing psychological distress.

When the evaluation is complete, observation and treatment can proceed on a twenty-four-hour-a-day schedule. Individual, group, and family therapy are usually included.

Therapeutic Communities.

These residential rehab centers are often run by ex-addicts. They emphasize group approaches and no-holds-barred confrontations with addicts. No drug use whatsoever is allowed.

The counselors seek to compel addicts to face up to their own immaturity and irresponsibility and to stop running away from reality. Addicts share responsibility for maintaining the center, performing all the necessary chores. They are expected to keep their own areas and themselves neat and clean at all times.

A stay in this type of facility can be extremely stressful. It is not recommended for a patient's first experience in rehabilitation, but it seems to work well with patients who have experienced other forms of treatment.

A relatively recent form of residential treatment for teenagers is the so-called "Toughlove" type. Teens committed to these centers face harsher discipline than elsewhere. Confrontations with staff members are sometimes demeaning, and punishment for the slightest infractions of the rules can be severe. Some graduates of these centers praise them highly, but others have accused them of brutality and in some instances have sued for damages.

Two particularly successful therapeutic communities, Phoenix House and Daytop Village, are discussed in detail later in this chapter.

Halfway Houses.

These are another type of residential center. They are intended for addicts undergoing outpatient treatment, or for those nearing discharge from another drug program, or for those living in a home environment unfavorable to successful rehabilitation. Most halfway houses offer less rigorous treatment than other drug residences, but they do provide a structured setting where the patient can accustom himself to a drug-free life-style before returning to life outside.

"Anonymous" Groups.

These include Alcoholics Anonymous and all its offshoots, such as Narcotics Anonymous, Cocaine Anonymous, and Alanon. They operate on the basis of AA's famous "twelve-step" method. Basically they require addicts to admit their problem publicly, to place their faith in any higher spiritual power that they acknowledge, to recognize that they can make no trustworthy long-term commitment to quit, and to pledge to struggle against their addictions "one day at a time."

Addicts attending "Anonymous" meetings benefit from seeing that others face the same problems that they do. They learn to give compassionate support to other members and receive it from them. They are never considered cured. They must keep attending meetings regularly for the rest of their lives.

An important consideration for many addicts is that these organizations charge nothing for attending their meetings.

A recent survey found that 29 percent of members of "Anonymous" groups stay sober or drug-free for over five years, while 38 percent do so for one to five years. These results are about average for drug treatment programs.

The "Anonymous" programs have been criticized for not requiring that addicts stop drinking or taking drugs before they are admitted to meetings or even that they stop while attending.

However, addicts in "Anonymous" meetings are prohibited from "sharing" if they have taken a mind-altering substance in the twenty-four-hour period before the meeting. They use the "one day at a time" concept and peer pressure to enforce abstinence.

Acupuncture.

This treatment was originally developed in China. It has been used there for many centuries to treat a wide variety of afflictions and as an anaesthetic. Western medical scientists have found it safe and effective and are increasingly adapting it to their own uses. As used with drug addicts, needles are inserted painlessly at certain points in the ear or hand. The treatment is given every day for at least ten days. Patients continue to receive it less frequently for several months while attending "Anonymous" meetings. Although no scientific studies have yet been completed, preliminary indications are that the treatment blocks the craving for crack, cocaine, and heroin. It costs only fifteen dollars per treatment and could become a viable alternative to more expensive modes.

More than 3,000 crack addicts have been treated with acupuncture at Kings County and Lincoln hospitals in New York. A study showed that at least 50 percent of those ordered by the criminal justice system to take the treatment were able to stay free of crack for at least two months.

At a hearing in New York's City Hall, Dr. Michael Smith of Lincoln Hospital's acupuncture-detoxification unit was asked about the technique's effectiveness. "When you've got a fellow with a gun in his pocket," he replied, "and he's looking for methadone, and you say to him, 'No, wait, we'll do this instead'—you'd better be good."

Methadone Maintenance.

Methadone is a synthetic narcotic that blocks the craving for heroin and has a calming effect. It sets up its own addiction, however.

The drug is taken orally, usually mixed with orange drink. Most doses are taken at clinics under the direct observation of a staff member. Some patients may also be given take-home bottles for self-administration. Each dose costs fifteen dollars, making this one of the least expensive modes of treatment. Addicts who cannot afford even that amount usually arrange with a social worker to get the drug free. Unlike heroin, which has to be taken every four to six hours, methadone only has to be taken once a day, as its effects last for twenty-four hours.

Methadone was developed in the early 1960s at Rockefeller Institute. Its introduction was accompanied by a great deal of fanfare. It was hailed as a "miracle" antidote for heroin. Addicts taking methadone avoided the stupefying effects of the heroin high and were able to function in society.

The hope was that addicts going on methadone programs would gradually be stabilized and get their lives under control. They could then be weaned from methadone and live drug-free lives. Crime rates associated with heroin use would supposedly drop sharply.

Today New York City runs an $80-million-a-year methadone program, the nation's largest. It treats 31,000 heroin junkies. But this hopeful alternative form of treatment has proved a disappointment. An estimated 60 percent of those taking methadone actively abuse other drugs. Most smoke crack and shoot cocaine into their veins.

A methadone black market is booming, often right outside the doors of methadone clinics. Thousands of patients and others buy and sell take-home doses for thirty-five dollars a bottle. The money is almost always used for drugs other than heroin. Their effects are not blocked by methadone.

New York has recorded an estimated 200 methadone-related overdose deaths a year. Most result from use of the drug in combination with others.

Many methadone patients stay hooked on the drug for as long as ten to fifteen years. Some experts insist that it must be taken for life. Some states allow patients to keep taking it for no more than two years. They rely much more heavily on drug-free forms of treatment like those discussed above.

Of the 260,000 Americans currently enrolled in publicly funded addiction clinics, about one-third are receiving methadone treatment in New York. They are mostly poor and members of minority groups. Those who can afford to, enroll in private clinics using drug-free modes of treatment. The nation's addict-treatment system operates in two tiers, set apart by income and social standing.

In the 1960s, when methadone treatment was first licensed by the federal government, the clinics were required to provide a full range of counseling and social services along with the drug. That added to the expense and cut down on the number of addicts that could be treated. New York's clinics were so overcrowded that little counseling could actually be offered.

In 1987 the government gave New York's Beth Israel Hospital, a leader in methadone maintenance, permission to dispense the drug to addicts on waiting lists without all the services. They were to get only a physical exam and counseling about AIDS transmission (many were using needles to take other drugs). The program was carefully monitored, with all doses taken under supervision.

The addicts' use of needles declined, and their quality of life improved. The government is considering expanding the system to nationwide use. The prime objective is to combat the rapidly spreading AIDS epidemic.

Used in closely supervised environments, says Dr. Marvin Snyder, a research expert with NIDA,

> methadone works, depending on your definition of success. In terms of holding jobs, maintaining family relationships, having clean urines for opiate drugs and decreasing the use of needles and the potential spread of AIDS, methadone is a very successful drug. But the problem is that many clinics aren't using it appropriately.

Lamont Timmins, a thirty-seven-year-old addict who has been on methadone for five years, told *Newsday* that it ended his heroin abuse, helped him to avoid AIDS, and enabled him to keep his job as a hospital nurse.

> It helped me. I'm in school. It got me off drugs. I never miss my methadone. It's like missing your shot of insulin as a diabetic. Your body is used to it. And if you don't take it, you go through withdrawal.

Wide disagreement exists about the relative merits of methadone and drug-free treatment. A number of studies show that fewer than 10 percent of patients who graduate from methadone programs stay drug-free. Yet some experts claim that even lower percentages of graduates of drug-free programs stay "clean."

Medications for Cocaine.

Considerable effort has been and is being devoted to the search for a drug that would block the effects of cocaine. Results have been limited so far.

Drugs usually employed to treat depression help some users to stop taking cocaine during the first phase of their addiction, when the craving is at its most overwhelming. These drugs blunt the cocaine high. But they do not work on all users, as methadone does on all heroin junkies. They are more effective on cocaine users than on crack addicts.

Numerous other types of drugs are still in the testing stage.

PHOENIX AND DAYTOP

Phoenix House and Daytop Village are two of the most respected and successful therapeutic communities.

The former was founded in 1967 in New York by a group of young heroin addicts. Unable to find suitable treatment in the established system, they pooled their welfare checks and began to develop their own program. It was based on hard physical labor, group encounters, and a drug-free environment. They adopted the name "Phoenix" because that is the name of the mythical bird that died and arose out of its own ashes.

Today the Phoenix House Foundation operates six treatment centers in New York State and four in California. It treats about a thousand addicts in New York. Patients as young as fourteen are admitted. Phoenix House also develops drug-education curricula for public and private schools all over the U.S.

The Phoenix program takes a minimum of eighteen months. Addicts are required to detoxify (stop taking drugs) before they can be admitted. They must remain drug-free throughout their stay.

Once admitted, the newcomers are relegated to the most menial jobs: cleaning toilets, mopping, sweeping, serving meals, etcetera. The work is regarded as an essential part of their therapy.

Older residents can interrupt them at any time to quiz them on house rules and regulations. Breaking any of these can lead to loss of a higher-status job in the house, losing weekend leaves, or even expulsion. One long-time resident who had sneaked out to cop some crack was required to sit in a hallway and try for days to explain to other residents, one at a time, why he had violated everything that Phoenix House had tried to teach him.

With good behavior, patients gradually work their way up to higher levels of responsibility. At the same time, they receive counseling and participate in group encounter sessions.

One resident lost her temper and cursed at a staff member. She had previously earned a desirable job at the Phoenix House induction center. For three and a half months, she had been helping to screen new residents and prepare them for their lives at the center. Now she suddenly found herself demoted back to the lowly service crew. But she was still permitted to offer advice to less experienced residents. "I didn't realize what I had learned in three and a half months [at the induction center]," she told a *New York Times* reporter. "Now I cry. I want to get back outside and work."

Most Phoenix residents are between the ages of twenty and forty. They come from a wide range of social and economic backgrounds, but almost all are now financially broke as a result of their addictions. Fifteen percent were convicted of drug offenses and remanded to the center through the criminal justice system.

"You've lost everything when you've got to come here," said one recovering crack addict. "You've hit rock bottom. This place is no resort at all."

This type of treatment can be expensive, costing an average of $15,000 a year. But many residents pay little or nothing, depending on their incomes.

Not surprisingly in view of the expense, strict discipline, and stressful confrontations, dropout rates are high. They range around the 60 percent mark. But supporters of such programs point out that more of their graduates tend to remain drug-free than do those of other programs.

Daytop Village, Inc., is the largest and oldest drug program in the U.S. The original name for Daytop Village was "Drug Addicted Youth in Treatment on Probation." The acronym has yielded a slogan for Daytop residents: "Drug Addicts Yielding to Persuasion." It has eight outreach and eight residential centers in New York State and several elsewhere across the U.S. Its mode of operation is generally similar to that of Phoenix House.

It was cofounded in 1963—and it is still headed—by sixty-five-year-old Monsignor William B. O'Brien, a former parish priest who is now the recognized leader of the worldwide movement to set up drug-free residential rehab centers. More than fifty countries have such programs.

Daytop, like other residential centers, still runs into opposition whenever it tries to expand. Residents of neighborhoods where a new branch is planned fear increased crime and vandalism, as well as lowered property values. Yet none of the Daytop centers has ever caused either. The program is acknowledged a good neighbor everywhere.

This is no accident. The program is so highly structured and carefully monitored that the residents have little time or opportunity to indulge in criminal behavior. The only incidents that occurred close to one Daytop center were committed by outside addicts who had smashed Daytop cars and robbed the center at night. "We have been the victims there," said Monsignor O'Brien, "not the community."

Why do therapeutic communities work at all? Says Douglas Chiappetta, director of Therapeutic Communities of America: "They are not just dealing with the drug addiction, but with the reason that drives that person to use drugs."

EVALUATING TREATMENTS

Experience has shown that there is little, if any, difference in the long-term effectiveness of expensive inpatient programs and far less costly outpatient ones. Inpatient treatment should probably be reserved mainly for patients whose addiction is intertwined with psychiatric problems.

Parents are usually advised to enroll their children in programs specifically designed for adolescents. Teens have their own unique set of personal, social, and family problems. They respond best to groups consisting of their peers and to therapists and counselors who understand and can empathize with young people.

At the same time, parents need to exercise care in committing   al, clinic, or residential
doned and stigmatized
ber of teens committed
ly in recent years. The
v suggests that greater
eatment for teenagers.
best to drug treatment,
chool or work records,
ommitting themselves
ife, have better-than-
hers who face severe
s, such as divorce, job
new sources of hope
py, new love relation-

weapons available for
a part of the nation's
how much to other
ecome a major politi-
e of several recent

****
Newhope Library Learning Center
11/4/2003 5:05:44 PM
****

Substance abuse /

31994009536761
Due: 11/18/2003 11:59:00 PM

Drugs, society & human behavior /
Ray, Oakley Stern
31994010866504
Due: 11/18/2003 11:59:00 PM

Drugged America /
Harris, Jonathan
31994007898692
Due: 11/18/2003 11:59:00 PM

10

Who Is Winning the War on Drugs?

On September 5, 1989, President George Bush proposed the most far-reaching antidrug plan in the nation's history. The drug crisis, he said, was "the gravest domestic threat facing our nation today." His plan raised federal antidrug funding to an unprecedented total of $7.9 billion for the fiscal year 1990. Larger expenditures were planned for the ensuing years.

Congress later added another $1.1 billion for the first year. The president's plan had allotted 70 percent of the funds for law enforcement and 30 percent for prevention, education, and treatment. The added funds were earmarked exclusively for the latter purposes.

Although the president's plan was larger and bolder than any put forth by his predecessor, Ronald Reagan, only $717 million was actually new funding. Bush had already proposed the other appropriations in earlier budget and anticrime messages.

PRESIDENT BUSH'S WAR

Bush's plan more than doubled grants for state and local law enforcement. It provided governments of cocaine-producing countries with sharply increased funding to battle drug traffickers. It laid out big increases for treatment programs.

As part of a new drive aimed at cutting down demand for drugs, Bush urged the states to launch a campaign against recreational and casual drug users. He suggested several possible penalties, including suspensions of drivers' licenses and loss of government permits and benefits, including college loans. For nonviolent offenders, such new ideas as house arrest and boot camp were suggested to avoid further crowding of the nation's already bursting prisons.

In November 1990, a new federal law was passed reducing highway aid to states that do not suspend driver's licenses of all persons convicted of drug-related crimes. The law takes effect in 1993.

The Bush program also established civil fines of up to $10,000 for "possession of small amounts of certain controlled substances." This measure would do away with the need for trials in minor cases of simple possession.

A number of prosecutors have protested against the anti-user provisions of the new law. Prosecution staffs are already overloaded with more serious cases involving top-level dealers and large quantities of drugs. They would need to be vastly expanded to pursue the thousands of lesser cases.

Under the new plan, drug testing was to be expanded to cover all persons under the control of state criminal justice systems. These include parolees, prisoners, and people out on bail. States that declined would lose federal funds. This provision was later rejected by the Senate.

The area that received the largest single amount of funding, $1.6 billion, was the expansion and construction of federal prisons. State officials complained that the plan provided only minimal funds for their prisons. State and local prisons, commented Governor Mario Cuomo of New York, "hold the vast majority of inmates convicted of drug-related crimes."

Cuomo was particularly outraged by the amount allotted to state and local law enforcement:

> *Did you say $200 million? For all the states? And all the cities? And all the police forces? And all the prisons? And all the courts? And all the judges? And all the prosecutors? Don't tell me $200 million. Say zero!*

Former secretary of Health, Education, and Welfare Joseph A. Califano Jr. criticized the president's plan for skimping on research. A mere $500 million for this purpose was utterly inadequate:

> *This includes the hunt for heroin substitutes less debilitating than methadone and new drugs to relieve the craving for cocaine and crack . . . understanding alcoholism, multiple addiction and the genetics and psychology of addiction; and developing effective prevention and treatment programs.*

Califano recommended an appropriation of at least $1 billion for basic research and the establishment of an institute on addiction among the National Institutes of Health.

The president's plan was the product of six months of work by a government agency created in 1988 under the Reagan administration, the National Drug Control Policy Board. Reagan had appointed former secretary of Education William J. Bennett to head it. Bennett was immediately dubbed the nation's "drug czar" by the media. He told reporters that the plan's main goal was to reduce drug use by Americans. The primary focus was to be demand, not supply. "Yes," he said, "we are going to come down hard on the casual user."

Underlying the new plan was the alarm felt by large numbers of Americans over the worsening drug crisis. Public-opinion polls have shown that many are sufficiently concerned to favor tough action, even at the cost of serious infringements on civil liberties. Some Americans are ready, for example, to permit searches without warrants of their homes, to inform on drug-abusing members of their own families, and to permit use of the armed forces to patrol their neighborhoods.

Defenders of civil liberties argue that the prevalence of such opinions reflects a failure of the American education system and the media. They feel that the general public is insufficiently informed about the rights and protections written into the Constitution by the Founding Fathers.

Bush's declaration of a war on drugs was the latest in a long series of antidrug campaigns announced by previous presidents. Starting at least as far back as the administration of Dwight D. Eisenhower in the 1950s, every president has ordered increasingly drastic antidrug measures.

The AntiDrug Abuse Act of 1988, for example, passed during the Reagan administration, established the cabinet-level post of Director of the National Drug Control Policy Board. It also decreed the death penalty for drug traffickers who commit murders and for anyone who kills a police officer in the course of a drug-related crime. Proposals were later put forth to impose the death penalty on all major traffickers.

Bush's new plan was the most ambitious ever proposed. "This scourge [of drugs] will end," he had promised in his inaugural address. He set "victory over drugs" as his goal.

But he had hardly finished speaking before members of his own administration were admitting to reporters that that victory could probably not be reached in this generation. They put forward two more modest and realistic goals. One was to get the problem of hard-core addiction under some degree of control. The other was to hasten the current national decline in drug use by occasional users.

Campaigns aimed at hard-core addicts would mostly affect the poorer classes and minorities. Success would undoubtedly depend on solving, or at least easing, the complicated social and economic problems besetting these groups.

Life magazine (September 1989) saw the lack of attention to these problems as the "fundamental flaw" in the drug war: "In the streets of America's cities the police are being asked to solve what is at heart a social problem."

But antipoverty programs were not high on the agenda of the Bush administration. "We have been fighting such social ills for decades," Bennett wrote in his report to the president outlining the plan. "We need not—and cannot—sit back and wait for that fight to be won for good."

Bennett told an interviewer he believes "the best defense against drugs are . . . good family, good schools, good churches."

Striving to reduce occasional use would mostly affect the middle and upper classes. Declining drug use by nonaddicted members of these groups already shows the beneficial effects of ongoing antidrug education programs, publicity campaigns, and society's growing intolerance for drugs.

Specifically, the new war on drugs set as its two-year goal a reduction of 10 percent in the number of people reporting that they had used drugs during the previous month. Over ten years, the hoped-for reduction would increase to 50 percent. In actuality, a NIDA survey taken only weeks before the plan was announced had already indicated a 37 percent drop in occasional drug use since 1979.

Some of the most potent weapons in the war against drugs are the recently enacted laws authorizing seizure of property used in drug-related activities or acquired with funds gained from such activities. Federal, state, and local law-enforcement agencies have seized property worth millions—from real estate to cars, planes, trucks, and ships—not to mention large amounts of hard cash. Funding for law enforcement has benefited enormously; the total value of the assets seized rose from $200 million in 1985 to about $1 billion during 1989.

Seizures of narcotics have also increased dramatically. From 1982 until the end of 1989, cocaine seizures soared from about 12,000 pounds to over 181,000 pounds, while heroin seizures went from a mere 515 pounds to nearly 1.75 million pounds. Only marijuana seizures have declined, dropping from 2,400,000 pounds in 1982 to a little more than 700,000 pounds in 1989.

Notwithstanding these generally impressive figures, drug supplies remain abundant throughout the U.S.

In 1988 the government announced a "zero tolerance"

policy. Any vehicle found with any amount of illegal drugs, no matter how minute, would be seized. The value of the seizures based on this policy was immense. But the government was blocked in the case of the $2.5 million private yacht *Ark Royal.* It was seized when less than one-tenth of an ounce of marijuana was discovered on board. A court found that this evidence was insufficient to prove the boat was involved in smuggling, and it had to be returned to its owners.

The seizure policy can sometimes arouse fierce local resentments. A troubling example is the case of Robert Machin, a Vermont farmer. In the fall of 1988, the Vermont State Police got a tip that Machin was growing 200 marijuana plants on his forty-nine-acre farm. When the police raided the place, they found only a dozen plants, many of them too dry to be of any value.

Machin pleaded guilty and was sentenced to perform fifty hours of community service. There was no evidence that he had ever intended to sell any of the crop. But then federal marshals seized the farm. The local people, including several elected officials, were outraged. State legislator Stephen Webster spoke for many: "The imposition of this penalty is much too severe." The final outcome awaits the result of a federal civil suit as of this writing.

In March 1990, only months after the president presented his antidrug plan, the State Department issued a dismaying report. It indicated that the worldwide problem was worsening despite all the U.S. had tried to do.

The report disclosed that global production of opium poppies, coca, marijuana, and hashish had soared in 1989. So did drug abuse around the world, as drug traffickers aggressively sought new markets for the increased supply.

The State Department noted some successes, such as

the capture of record amounts of drugs, the imprisonment of major traffickers, and the seizure of millions of dollars worth of drug smugglers' assets. Several countries signed new treaties of antidrug cooperation, and tough new laws were passed against money laundering.

But the failures far overshadowed the successes. The report's overall tone was pessimistic:

> *Worldwide narcotics production reached new levels, corruption undermined enforcement efforts, and a number of governments still failed to exhibit a serious commitment to reducing drug production and trafficking.*

There were also signs of trouble in the war on drugs within the U.S. Shortly after his appointment as national drug policy adviser, William J. Bennett had singled out drug-infested Washington, D.C., as "a test case." It was to be the first of several cities slated to undergo a concentrated cleanup by several law-enforcement agencies working in tandem.

But a year later, in April 1990, he issued a report admitting failure. Illegal drugs were still plentiful in the nation's capital, and the homicide rate showed no sign of a decrease.

Bennett resigned in November 1990. His supporters credited him with bringing about some decline in drug use, especially in casual and recreational use. But hard-core addiction in the nation's inner cities remained high, and drug-related violence was increasing. President Bush named Bob Martinez, former governor of Florida, to succeed Bennett.

Still another distressing judgment came from Admiral Paul A. Yost, Jr., commandant of the Coast Guard, in testimony before a congressional committee early in 1990. Asked what percentage of the cocaine coming into the U.S. the authorities had been able to seize in 1989, he gave an estimate of approximately 3 percent. Yost was then asked how much federal money would have to be spent to interdict 50 percent of the incoming cocaine. He replied that there wasn't enough money in the entire federal budget to do that.

Pressure from an aroused public and from vote-seeking politicians has compelled law-enforcement authorities to produce ever-mounting numbers of drug arrests. The effect has been havoc for our criminal justice system. The problem was dramatically highlighted by American Broadcasting Corporation newsman Ted Koppel on a September 1990 broadcast of his nightly TV program, *Nightline.*

"There are too many people," Koppel commented, "being jammed through a system that was overburdened before the war on drugs began." In New York City alone, there were 50,000 felony drug defendants in 1989. If all had insisted on their right to a jury trial, the cost would have added up to an estimated $6 billion.

Instead, most were persuaded to "plea bargain," which means that they gave up their right to a jury trial and pleaded guilty to a lesser charge. They then faced the likelihood of serving a much shorter sentence than they might have served if convicted by a jury.

"The trial by jury for people accused of drug-related felonies," said Koppel, "is on the verge of becoming an unaffordable luxury." Only 3 percent of felony drug cases ever go to trial.

"Like all wars," Koppel concluded, "the war on drugs is producing some unintended casualties. The legal system is one of them."

But law enforcement has recorded some noteworthy achievements. In April 1990, the FBI revealed the successful outcome of a long-term undercover operation known as "Cat-com," for catch communications. By patiently planting informers inside the drug gangs and amassing large quantities of evidence through electronic eavesdropping and other means, the FBI broke up seven Colombian drug rings in two years and netted sixty-eight persons. The information gathered by the FBI included the startling news that 200 other Colombian rings were operating within the U.S. or along the borders, more than had been believed before Cat-com began.

A WAR THE U.S. CANNOT WIN?

Notable among the leading critics of President Bush's plan was Congressman Charles B. Rangel. He was one among many who denounced the funding proposed by the president as inadequate in view of the vastness of the problem. *Time* magazine called it "laughably inadequate." Rangel even argued that the plan's goals were "like being half pregnant—winning 50 percent of the war."

Others estimated that even a limited effort, like fully funding treatment programs for children under sixteen, for youths currently in the juvenile justice system, and for pregnant addicts, would cost $3.9 billion. That was four times the amount the administration planned to spend for all forms of treatment.

The idea of substantially increasing the funds available for the drug war faced at least one major stumbling block: It was hard to see how it could be done unless taxes were raised. But President Bush had been elected partly because of his often-repeated campaign promise not to do that. He eventually approved some tax increases.

Bush explained the limited funding he had ordered for the drug war: "I have this overwhelming problem of the deficit to contend with." With the government already hundreds of billions of dollars in debt, he insisted that more liberal funding would worsen the already grave fiscal problem.

A number of observers have challenged the very notion of a war on drugs. Two University of Arizona professors, Michael Gottfredson and Travis Hirschi, have flatly declared that "the hard-line programs proposed by the president [would] have little impact on the crime rate or the drug problem." They pointed to federal Bureau of Justice statistics which show that expenditures for criminal justice in the last few years have increased four times as rapidly as for education and twice as rapidly as for health and hospitals.

Editor-author Barbara Ehrenreich, writing in *Ms.* magazine (November 1988), denounced what she saw as a national "drug frenzy." She noted that tobacco—a legal drug—kills over 300,000 people a year. Alcohol—also legal—kills 100,000, including victims of drunk drivers. All the illicit drugs that are the targets of so much public condemnation and expense kill a total of around 3,000.

In March 1990, the National Association of State Alcohol and Drug Abuse Directors released a report that sharply criticized President Bush's policy of favoring law enforcement over prevention, education, and treatment. The policy was not "cost-effective," the report said, pointing out that every dollar spent on treatment brought a gain of $11.54 to society by reducing such related costs as crime and prison beds.

Dr. Peter Pinto, clinical director of Samaritan Village, Inc., a residential drug-free therapeutic community in New

York, offered these figures comparing some costs related to drug abuse and treatment:

- the cost of keeping someone in prison varies from $25,000 through $50,000 per inmate annually;

- the cost of AIDS treatment runs as high as $100,000 per patient annually.

Compare the costs of:

- $3,000 per year for methadone maintenance treatment programs;

- $2,300 for outpatient treatment;

- $15,000 for inpatient treatment.

An ex-addict named Mike Posey challenged the drug war on provocative grounds in a recent *New York Times* article. He had abused drugs for twenty years:

> *Nothing worked to get me to stop all that behavior except just plain being sick and tired. Nothing. No threats, not ten-plus years in prison. . . . I used until I got through. Period. And that's when you'll win the war. When all the dope fiends are done. Not a minute before.*

Real addicts, Posey wrote, will keep using till they die, or go crazy, or go to jail. And there are plenty of drugs available in jail.

> *One day, though, if you live, there comes the time when it doesn't work anymore. . . . The feeling is harder to get and harder to keep chasing. You've gotten old.*

Posey was forty when he quit. Considering the number of addicts who have quit at earlier ages after going through some form of treatment, or even on their own or with the support of friends and family, his pessimism seems extreme.

Perhaps the broadest critique of the war on drugs was that of Professor Arnold Trebach, director of the Drug Policy Foundation in Washington, D.C. He denounces our drug laws as irrational and unscientific. They are out of touch with millions of Americans, and that makes them unenforceable, he said.

The laws make no clear distinctions. They criminalize moderate, occasional drug users—anywhere from 20 to 40 million Americans—as well as serious abusers.

All talk about "winning" the drug war or attaining a "drug-free" America, says Trebach, is empty rhetoric. In view of the numbers of Americans who use drugs, the best we can hope for is to reduce drug abuse, not to eliminate it.

Trebach suggests an approach he calls "drug peace" in the place of drug war. He opposes the prevalent hostile and punitive approach to addicts. He favors dealing with them calmly, without hate or fear. They should not be lumped together and all handled in the same way, but treated in ways that suit individual differences.

Trebach is a leading advocate of affordable treatment on demand. While in treatment, addicts should be persuaded to sign contracts in which they pledge to lead productive, non-criminal lives.

All drugs are dangerous, Trebach admits. But there are individuals who use them safely, moderately, as responsibly as it is possible to do. As long as they remain fully capable of functioning in society and do not try to seduce others into drug use, these people should not be targets of detection and punishment.

Police work, says Trebach, should concentrate on violent criminals and the organized mobs that dominate and profit the most from the drug trade. He feels that the vast efforts expended on arrests of street-level dealers and their customers are futile and unnecessary.

Peter Reuter, a prominent analyst at the Rand Corporation —a leading "think tank"—offers another challenge to Bush's plan. The "war on drugs" placed primary emphasis on interdiction, or stopping the flow of drugs across the borders. Enormous efforts in this sphere have as yet yielded disappointing results, intercepting perhaps 10 percent of the influx.

Reuter's computer projections show that even if the interdiction rate ever reached as high as 40 percent, it would do little to cut drug availability. He considers interdiction merely a form of tax on the smugglers. The cost is passed on to the consumer, guaranteeing the smugglers' profits.

Statistics lend credibility to Reuter's beliefs. For instance, the U.S. government spent more than $10 billion on law enforcement aimed at cocaine smuggling from 1980 to 1988. Yet the supply of cocaine in the country multiplied by ten. Coca fields in the Andes expanded by 25 percent. In 1980, a kilo of cocaine cost $60,000 wholesale in Miami. In 1988, it cost $10,000.

Reuter also criticizes the U.S. effort to persuade other countries to cut production of crops like coca, opium poppies, and marijuana plants. Our insistence has sometimes created friction between the U.S. and its friends abroad. In any case, the policy has so far been a failure. World production has increased. As a result, drug prices in the U.S. have steadily gone down and drug use has risen.

Most producing countries have neither the motivation nor the means to reduce the cultivation of drugs. They, and large sections of their farm populations, have become dependent on the substantial incomes these crops bring in.

Colombia is a noteworthy example of a country that has made a genuine effort to cooperate. Its campaigns against the drug lords and their laboratories have plunged it into a virtual civil war. Violence ordered by the drug lords has terrorized the entire country. The final outcome is far from certain.

U.S. Senator Daniel Patrick Moynihan advocates getting tough with drug-producing countries. We should furnish any countries that refuse to take serious measures to cut production with "no arms, no aid, no loan rescheduling, no anything."

THE DEBATE OVER USE OF THE MILITARY

By the early 1980s, it was obvious that the war on drugs was far from being won. The drug traffickers seemed to be the only real winners so far.

The never-ending search for new and more effective ways to fight the drug war produced a number of proposals. One that quickly won influential support favored deploying the armed forces against the drug traffickers.

This could only be done if a federal law known as the Posse Comitatus Act were amended. It specifically forbade the use of military forces to aid law enforcement within the U.S. Amendments added in 1982 did away with this prohibition, although the law still placed certain limits on the military's role.

Under the amended law, no members of the armed forces could intercept or arrest drug traffickers. They could be used in training, intelligence gathering, and detection. Servicemen could also operate military equipment for civilian law-enforcement agencies.

A partial solution was suggested early in 1989 in the form of a decision to use National Guard units for drug assignments instead of the regular armed forces. Restrictions on the use of federal troops to support local law enforcement do not apply to the Guard, which is under the control of the states. But the Guard can only be assigned to law-enforcement duties inside the U.S.

The assignment went to such highly trained National Guard units as helicopter squadrons and military police detachments. They were deemed well suited for detecting smuggling operations and transporting law-enforcement officers to intercept them. The Guard would also lend specialized equipment to the officers, such as night-vision goggles, helicopters, small arms, and bulletproof vests.

The Guard was ordered to make antidrug activities as important as training for combat. But it would limit itself to assisting lawmen. Its soldiers would neither patrol the streets nor arrest drug suspects nor handle any drugs. Its training centers would not be used for storing contraband.

The Guard's duties would include surveillance and tracking of smugglers and assistance with customs searches of shipping containers but not of people.

In September 1989, Secretary of Defense Richard Cheney ordered all military commanders to prepare plans for a major campaign against drug trafficking outside the U.S. "The Department of Defense," Cheney wrote, "will assist in the attack on production of illegal drugs at the source." Soon afterward Attorney-General Richard Thornburgh issued a formal legal opinion declaring that the Posse Comitatus Act limitations did not apply to actions by the military overseas.

Some of the military equipment to be used in the drug war was among the finest available. It included the Bell 200 "Cobra" assault helicopter, for example. This was the fastest and most heavily armed such craft in existence. Also placed at the disposal of law enforcement was the Navy's EC-2 radar plane, capable of detecting other aircraft at distances of up to a hundred miles; "Fat Albert," a fleet of surveillance balloons with sophisticated radar and listening devices; NASA satellites; and U.S. Customs Service "Blue Thunder" vessels, designed to outrun the traffickers' fastest boats.

Proposals to deploy U.S. armed forces to combat drug trafficking in countries overseas provoked intense debate. In September 1989, President Bush signed a top-secret national security directive setting forth guidelines for such use of the military. It specified that they would never be sent abroad unless the country concerned specifically requested it. They would function only as "advisers," to assist with training the area's armed forces.

Drug czar William Bennett had assured reporters that the administration had no intention of embroiling U.S. forces in a drug war in the jungles of South America. But only one month later, *Army Times* was reporting that "despite denials by the Bush administration the U.S. forces have a direct combat role in the fight against South American cocaine cartels. Army Special Operations Forces [the famous Green Berets] boast that they are on the front lines in the escalating war against drugs."

A Green Beret master sergeant explained the U.S. involvement: "It is very difficult to properly train these armies to perform long-range recon [reconnaissance] patrols for drug targets without supervising them on at least their first few missions."

Another *Army Times* article found similarities to the Vietnam War in the situation in the jungles of South America. One Vietnam veteran saw clear parallels in a newly constructed antidrug base at Santa Lucia in Peru's Upper

Huallaga Valley. It was "just like a firebase in Vietnam," with its guard towers, helicopter pad, land mines, concentric perimeters of barbed wire, and sandbagged fortifications. However, it has been manned entirely by U.S. civilians thus far.

The Santa Lucia base is located in one of the world's largest coca-growing areas, which supplies some 60 percent of U.S. demand. The valley is also controlled by the ultraradical Shining Path guerrillas. Armed conflict between these forces and the Americans is an ominous possibility.

U.S. officials reported a steady increase in the number of drug laboratories destroyed and acres of coca eradicated. But the ultimate value of the use of the military in South American antidrug operations has yet to be determined.

One of those who doubt the logic of these operations is retired Major General Wallace Nutting. From 1979 to 1983 he headed the Southern Command, which runs U.S. military activities in South America. "Combat skills," says Nutting, "are not always relevant to the drug problem. Most of the U.S. officer corps is quite leery" of this involvement.

U.S. personnel at the Santa Lucia base include only fifteen or fewer Drug Enforcement Administration agents. Operating with inadequate equipment, very limited training, and mixed orders from American and local officials, they are virtually prisoners. The base is surrounded by hostile hill countryside populated by peasants who depend on coca cultivation. The well-armed Shining Path guerrillas dominate the region.

The U.S. Navy announced that it was stationing an aircraft-carrier battle group off the coast of Colombia. The Colombians had not been consulted. They protested vehemently to the U.S. government about this "blockade." On January 16, 1990, the U.S. "postponed" deployment of the carrier force.

In the meantime, plans were announced for placing

ground-based radar units in the mountains of Bolivia, Colombia, and Peru. They could track planes suspected of carrying drugs. Installation of these units proceeded without hindrance.

There was considerable opposition within the military itself to these new assignments. Highly placed commanders felt that their forces were not properly trained nor intended for activities that were essentially police work. They argued that such a commitment would weaken the armed services by distracting them from their fundamental task of protecting national security.

The Bush administration has decided to strengthen anti-drug operations in the Andean region of South America as a whole and the Santa Lucia base in particular. Unspecified numbers of Special Forces troops will be sent into these areas. They have orders to avoid combat, but no one can predict how long they will be able to do that.

The government's efforts to cut down on the supply of drugs from abroad competes for funds and attention with efforts to reduce demand at home. To accomplish the latter goal, the government favors widespread adoption of drug testing.

11

To Test or Not to Test

Some 70 percent of illicit drug users are employed. Of Americans aged eighteen to twenty-five now entering the work force, 22 percent are current users of marijuana and 8 percent are users of cocaine. Advocates of drug testing insist that, both for safety reasons and to enhance productivity, the locations at which Americans work must be cleansed of drug use.

Former president Ronald Reagan repeatedly declared that an essential goal of the war against drugs is "drug-free workplaces." In 1986, Reagan set up a Commission on Organized Crime. One of its principal recommendations was for widespread drug testing, which is most commonly done by analyzing urine samples. (Blood tests are also used, though much less often.)

The commission recommended that federal agencies should test their employees and that federal contracts should not be granted to private companies that did not have testing programs. Other private companies, it maintained, should seriously consider testing.

GOVERNMENT TESTING AND PRIVATE TESTING

Public opinion stands massively in favor of wide testing. In a 1986 *USA Today* poll, fully 77 percent of those queried said they would not object to being tested at work. A poll taken at the end of 1989 found 55 percent in support of testing everyone. An overwhelming 67 percent favored testing all high-school students.

But requiring government employees to submit to drug tests raises grave constitutional issues. Urine samples must be produced in the presence of an observer, a clear infringement on individual privacy. The courts on several occasions have declared drug tests to be a form of search. Under the Fourth Amendment to the Constitution, the government is allowed to conduct only "reasonable" searches. These must be based on "probable cause," which means that there must be sufficient grounds for suspicion that a crime is either being committed or soon will be.

New York Times columnist William Safire gave eloquent expression to the feelings of many who oppose compulsory drug testing:

> *Not only is my home my castle, my body is my citadel. Unless I give you probable cause to suspect me of a crime, what goes on in my home and body and mind is my business.*

In 1987 the U.S. Department of Transportation ordered random drug testing of all of its employees whose jobs affect public safety, especially air traffic controllers. A year later the department extended the random testing order to 4 million nongovernment workers in transportation. The program covered 3 million interstate truck and bus drivers, as well as numerous airline pilots, navigators, flight attendants, and mechanics; railroad engineers, brakemen, and conductors; subway engineers and bus drivers in mass transit systems; seamen; and pipeline workers.

Unions, civil liberties groups, and others challenged the constitutionality of government-ordered testing without cause. They asserted that the tests violate constitutional guarantees of personal privacy. Other challenges were based on the contention that the tests were often unreliable. Testing programs, the unions argued, could be used to harass workers who for any reason might be considered troublesome to employers.

The American Civil Liberties Union suggested that neurological tests of pilots just before flights would make more sense than drug tests. The pilots could be examined quickly for visual acuity and motor coordination. Similar suggestions might apply to railroad engineers and truck drivers, among others.

ACLU lawyer Loren Siegel recommended reasonable observation of employees by supervisors and fellow workers. They could easily spot an impaired worker. "It's called the 'two-eyes test,'" she said.

A congressional report disclosed that of the railroad crews that had been involved in sixty accidents between January 1987 and November 1988, one in five had at least one member who tested positive for drugs. The question was whether such threats to the safety of the traveling public were adequate grounds for permitting searches without probable cause.

THE COURTS HAVE THEIR SAY

In a series of decisions, the Supreme Court ruled that certain circumstances can justify drug testing even where there is no probable cause to suspect drug abuse. Protecting the public's safety is one such circumstance. In March 1989, the Court specifically held that railway workers who had been involved in accidents or violations of safety rules could legally be tested for drugs. This decision was viewed as a landmark, opening the way for testing in many other transportation fields.

In another decision handed down at the same time, the Court ruled that U.S. Customs workers who applied for transfer or promotion to drug-enforcement jobs requiring them to carry a gun could also be tested. It was essential, the Court stated, to guarantee the integrity of workers engaged in any type of law enforcement—especially if their work brought them into contact with drugs.

Several months later, the Court upheld the random testing of the Boston police. Again, public safety and the officers' integrity were the deciding factors. The New York City Police Department, the largest in the nation, had already ordered random testing of its 26,000 officers.

The earlier ruling on testing railway workers was considerably broadened in May 1990, when another Supreme Court ruling allowed the government to test thousands of Department of Transportation employees in "sensitive" jobs. Nearly two-thirds are air-traffic controllers. Others include airplane mechanics, inspectors, and traffic-safety specialists.

In another 1990 decision, the justices refused to interfere with random drug tests for Justice Department employees with top security clearance and civilian drug and alcoholism counselors for the army.

The situation is different in private employment. These employees are not protected by the Constitution, which only limits acts by the government. The Bureau of Labor Statistics reported in January 1989 that 4 million pre-employment drug tests had already been conducted. Nearly 12 percent of the applicants had tested positive.

Some 17 million Americans work for employers who have testing programs. By 1992, the annual total of employees tested will probably rise to 22 million.

A California county court outlawed random testing of workers in private employment in 1988. Half a dozen other states passed laws restricting it. Then in June 1989, the Supreme Court upheld the right of railroads to test employees without first obtaining the agreement of the unions. The railroad involved was Conrail, a private employer. Shortly before, a crash involving Conrail locomotives and an Amtrak train had caused the deaths of sixteen people. The Conrail engineer had used marijuana.

The engineer, Ricky L. Gates, was sentenced to a five-year prison term on a state charge of manslaughter by locomotive, and in July 1988 he received an additional penalty of three years on a federal charge of conspiring to obstruct an investigation of the accident.

The decision seemed to bestow the Court's approval on the testing of thousands of transport workers in private employment—upholding the government's 1988 order affecting these workers.

On Long Island, N.Y., the board of education of the Patchogue-Medford school district ordered the testing of all probationary teachers. The New York Court of Appeals declared this order an unconstitutional search. There was no evidence of high levels of drug abuse among teachers to justify the testing program.

In a number of school districts, proposals have been put forward for testing students. Some proposals emphasized testing students taking part in extracurricular and athletic activities. They would be banned from such activities if they tested positive.

Piscataway High School, in New Jersey, sued for the right to search students and their possessions. The case involved a girl caught smoking in the bathroom. She denied she had been smoking. The assistant vice principal searched her purse and found a pack of Marlboro cigarettes, as well as pot-smoking equipment and notes indicating she might have been selling pot to other students. The girl's parents filed suit, claiming the search had violated the girl's Fourth Amendment rights.

The school took the case all the way to the Supreme Court. That body approved the search, even without a warrant, partly because of "school disorder [caused by] drug use and student crime."

Drug testing is rapidly becoming a big business. Laboratory revenues rose from $230 million in 1989 to an estimated $340 million in 1990. This was an impressive 48 percent jump.

On average, for tests run according to the tough federal rules, the labs charge $30 to $35 a person. Other tests cost slightly less. As the government certifies new labs, the increased competition will probably drive prices down.

TESTING IN THE ARMED FORCES

The biggest of all American testers is the armed forces. The services began testing for illegal drugs, but not for alcohol, in the late 1970s. About 3 million tests are administered to servicemen and -women each year. These are seldom based on evidence of impaired job performance.

The results claimed have been impressive. The Navy, for instance, claims that where 48 percent of its enlisted men were using drugs in 1982, that figure had gone down to a mere 4 percent by 1986. Performance was said to have improved in many categories. Fewer than 1 percent of Navy discharges were issued because of drugs. A shift from drugs to alcohol may explain the figures.

But in so massive a program, errors were almost inevitable. One Air Force officer testified in a court-martial that the lab at which he worked was producing false positives at the unacceptably high rate of 3 to 5 percent. He said that lab technicians were caught heating tacos in a glassware drying oven—causing abnormal and erroneous results.

In June 1984, the Army announced that it was mailing notices to almost 70,000 soldiers and ex-soldiers who had been victimized by false test results. The testing procedures had been found faulty, and the soldiers could all appeal, the Army told them. The Navy and Air Force made similar admissions.

QUESTIONS ABOUT TEST RESULTS

One of the most serious difficulties facing drug-test programs is the number of innocent substances that can give a "false positive" result. Poppy seeds, for instance, contain traces of morphine, though they have no effects on behavior. Eating three poppy-seed bagels can produce enough morphine in the body to result in a positive test.

Quinine is often used by drug dealers to dilute heroin. But it is also found in tonic water and some over-the-counter medications. Persons about to be tested would therefore be wise to avoid quinine.

Marijuana is sometimes used in cancer therapy. Opiates, the class of drugs to which heroin and morphine belong, are frequently used legitimately in sedatives, cough remedies, and painkillers. Cocaine is a powerful local anesthetic, often used in certain types of surgery. Anyone tested soon after using any of these drugs for legitimate purposes could be branded a drug abuser if the medical reasons for using the drug were unknown.

Drug tests also cannot tell exactly when a drug was taken. Marijuana, for instance, can be detected for many days after a single use. In cases of chronic use, it can be detected for as long as three weeks. Cocaine, on the other hand, is eliminated from the body rapidly. Two or three days after the last use, tests will give a negative result.

Nor can a test tell whether a drug has impaired a person's job performance. That person might have gotten "zonked" on some drug during the weekend but be perfectly fine at work on Monday morning. The test can only reveal whether or not a drug was taken.

Negative test results can also be inconclusive. They would not necessarily prove that an individual tested after an accident, for instance, was unimpaired at the time of the accident. The test will reveal nothing about safety hazards or other factors that might have affected the outcome.

Labs also vary in their precision. A sample labeled positive by one lab may be considered negative by another.

Still another complication is that the drugs people may be taking for valid medical reasons can crossreact with test ingredients, producing false positives. Many drugs commonly purchased for minor ailments without a prescription can have such results.

For tests to be at all reliable, they should be administered in two stages. A first, preliminary test will indicate if there is any grounds for suspicion. But this result should always be confirmed by a second test, using more refined and sophisticated techniques. The confirmatory methods now available have a very high degree of accuracy, but they are expensive. Even when they are used there is always a possibility of human error.

Drug war approaches such as drug testing, cracking down on users, and interdicting smuggling are only a few of the many that have been proposed by a wide variety of individuals and groups. They have not stopped the traffickers from winning the drug war so far.

A number of new proposals have been put forth. Some are unquestionably creative and innovative. They deserve consideration, if not acceptance.

12

Alternatives to War

Considering the frustrations and failures of the war on drugs, a number of distinguished Americans have urged that all drugs be legalized. Proponents of this approach include federal district judge Robert Sweet, former Secretary of State George Shultz, Mayor Kurt Schmoke of Baltimore, several congressmen, and two well-known spokesmen of conservatism, editor-columnist William F. Buckley and the Nobel Prize-winning economist Milton Friedman.

LEGALIZE ALL DRUGS, SOME, OR NONE?

Public opinion has repeatedly expressed opposition to the idea of legalizing drugs. In the most recent poll by the

National Opinion Research Center, fully five-sixths of those polled said marijuana should not be decriminalized. Decriminalization would mean that the legal penalties for possession of small amounts—for personal use—would be removed. Legalization would mean that the drug could be bought and sold openly, like any legal drug. Congress wrote its opposition into the 1989 AntiDrug Abuse Act, calling legalization an unjustified surrender in a war in which "there can be no substitute for total victory."

On the other side, George Shultz argued that "we should at least be willing to debate these issues." William F. Buckley predicted that legalization will "inevitably prevail because the alternatives have become increasingly discredited." Judge Sweet called the war on drugs a "bankrupt" policy.

Prolegalization advocates are convinced that the war against drugs cannot be won. They contend that the drug epidemic should be dealt with as a public-health problem, not a problem for the criminal justice system. The ban on drugs, they point out, only drives the prices up and feeds the traffickers' profits. It produces increasingly stringent law-enforcement measures that endanger the rights and liberties of Americans.

Some claim that the goal of a drug-free society is unattainable. More realistic goals, they contend, would include controlling drug use rather than prohibiting it and striving to reduce its harmful effects rather than eliminate them.

These advocates propose a variety of approaches. Some favor removing criminal penalties from marijuana on an experimental basis. Then, if this policy seems successful, other drugs could gradually be decriminalized as well. Others favor legalization of all drugs at once, even the most dangerous and addictive ones.

Without the astronomical profits of illegality, prolegalization advocates reason, the drug gangs and cartels would have to seek other moneymaking fields. The criminal activity and violence that surround the drug trade would shrink to more tolerable levels. The nation's cities could regain control of their streets.

The government would regulate the purity and potency of drugs available on the market. Accidental deaths due to poisonings and overdoses, so common now, would be reduced to near zero.

Legalization is also favored on the grounds that it would reduce the widespread corruption of law-enforcement officers. In the state of Georgia alone, at least eighty lawmen and public officials were charged with serious offenses, mostly accepting bribes, during the 1980s. In one noteworthy case, a state senator promised protection for drug smugglers if they helped finance his campaign for the state governorship.

The chief cause of police corruption is fairly obvious. Law enforcement is a relatively low-paid profession. Officers bearing heavy financial burdens find it hard to refuse offers that equal or surpass their yearly salary.

Proponents of legalization admit that drug abuse and addiction would probably increase at first, as drinking increased during the first decade after the repeal of Prohibition in 1933. But the extent of this increase cannot be predicted with any accuracy. This unknown quantity must be measured against the known social disasters that illegalization has caused.

The legalizers call for large-scale expansion of antidrug education and treatment programs. These would limit any increase in drug use. Eventually, they would reduce it.

As another method of fighting any increased drug use

that might result from legalization, warning labels would be placed on all drug containers. They would describe the specific dangers accompanying the use of each drug. Users would be reminded of the damage they were doing to themselves every time they removed a drug from its container. Labeling has already been found to be an effective step in the campaign against cigarette smoking.

Funds for these programs would be obtained from two sources. Drugs would be taxed, just as cigarettes and alcohol are. And billions now spent on futile attempts to enforce antidrug laws would be better spent on treatment and education.

Legalization would not mean that drugs would be obtainable by everyone. Under some legalization plans, addiction would be recognized as a disease. Drugs would then be made available to addicts only through licensed clinics. Dealing drugs outside the clinics would remain illegal. Addicts would receive counseling and other forms of therapy in a constant effort to get them to break their habit.

All advocates of legalization favor teaching the young not to start on drugs. Some add that those who do use them should be taught how to do so safely, moderately, and responsibly.

Congressman Rangel disagrees. He insists that no illicit drugs are safe. Antidrug education should emphasize rejection of all drugs and the reasons for it.

Like other opponents of legalization, Rangel challenges the idea that it would eliminate or even reduce crime. The repeal of Prohibition may have driven the mobs out of the liquor business, but they swiftly took control of other criminal pursuits. There is no reason to believe that the drug mobs would not do the same.

Even under a legalized system, the drug traffickers could produce cheaper and stronger narcotics than the law allowed. They would have plenty of customers, for many new ones would have been introduced to drugs and encouraged to try them by legalization.

Opponents of legalization point out that it would send the wrong signal to society in general and to the young in particular. Legalization would imply societal approval for immoral and destructive behavior. Children need a firm moral tradition on which to base their lives. They need to know what is right, decent, and responsible. Those who oppose legalization feel that children need to be impressed with the fact that drug abuse is evil, dangerous, a wrecker of families, and often fatal.

Although exact predictions of increased drug use after legalization may not be feasible, some experts believe that addiction would at least double. Dr. Robert Dupont, former chief of NIDA, believes that up to 50 million Americans would eventually use cocaine.

While it may be possible to imagine heroin addicts lining up for their drugs under a legal, regulated system (as many do now for methadone), no such prospect is imaginable for the millions caught up in the crack epidemic. Their craving is so strong and so constant that they cannot help indulging in it rather than nodding off regularly. There is no way they could be brought to use it in any reasonable fashion.

Crack also begets violence to a degree unmatched by any other drug. The steep rise in crack addiction among women has produced a sickening increase in child abuse. The stepped-up crack use that would almost certainly follow legalization would bring on inconceivable new waves of violence.

Legalization would benefit some segments of society while doing cruel damage to others. Those who do not use drugs might benefit from a reduction in crime. But addicts—and all those likely to become addicts under a legalized system—would be abandoned to their dependency. Psychiatrist Mitchell Rosenthal, president of Phoenix House Foundation, feels that the legalizers' reasoning is immoral, elitist, and racist. He says it amounts to "writing off hundreds and hundreds of thousands of people, their families and their children."

The most pitiable of these would be the new hosts of crack babies, born to the many thousands of female crack addicts who would be encouraged by legalization to buy and use the deadly drug. About 375,000 such infants were born in the U.S. in 1988.

In an article in the March 1990 issue of *Reader's Digest*, drug czar William Bennett summed up the arguments against legalization:

> *I find no merit in the legalizers' case. The simple fact is that drug use is wrong. And the moral argument, in the end, is the most compelling argument. . . .*
>
> *This war* can *be won. . . . This will not be easy. But the moral and social costs of surrender are simply too great to contemplate.*

FOCUS ON MARIJUANA

Marijuana is generally perceived to be the least harmful and least addictive of all illicit drugs. Some argue that it compares favorably with tobacco and alcohol, both of which are, of course, legal. Hence it is only natural that discussions of legalization give marijuana special attention.

Back in 1972, President Richard Nixon set up a commission to study the drug problem. Its recommendations included the decriminalization of marijuana. In 1982 a panel appointed by the National Academy of Sciences came to the same conclusion. Criminalizing marijuana, it stated, did more harm than good.

Between 60 and 70 million Americans have tried the drug. None has ever died of an overdose. Few ever become addicted to it. Most users continue to function as responsible citizens.

Arguing for its use in certain medical cases, an administrative law judge of the Drug Enforcement Administration concluded that, on the basis of the available evidence, marijuana "is one of the safest therapeutically active drugs known to man."

Seventeen states decriminalized marijuana during the 1970s. Despite opponents' predictions that use of the drug would skyrocket, use rates remained about the same as in other states. Where states have laws against possession of any amount, enforcement is generally lenient. Police and prosecutors feel their time and energies are better invested in going after more serious crimes. The inevitable result of having laws on the books that are seldom enforced is a lowering of respect for the law.

In those instances in which laws against marijuana have been strictly enforced, the results have sometimes been unfortunate. In the words of Harvard psychiatrist Lester Grinspoon:

> *When I visited Texas in 1972 I found that about 800 young people were in prison on marijuana charges . . . with an average sentence of almost ten years. Now, whatever our disagreements*

about the psychopharmacological effects of marijuana, no one claims it is as damaging as ten years in prison.

In a December 1988 editorial outlining the tasks awaiting newly appointed drug czar William Bennett, the *New York Times* firmly opposed the legalization of heroin and cocaine. But this staid and respectable newspaper added: "It might make sense to extend the decriminalizing of marijuana, which probably affects health less."

Decriminalization is also favored by Edward Brecher, one of the nation's most respected science writers and author of the widely used Consumers' Union book *Licit and Illicit Drugs* (1972). Brecher contends that the billions spent fighting marijuana use are wasted. Under proper regulation, marijuana might serve as a less dangerous substitute for alcohol.

The drug has been legal in Holland since the early 1970s. The Dutch feel that banning marijuana only places it under the control of criminals, who are all too eager to move their customers on to the use of hard drugs. A new law reduced the penalties for simple possession of small amounts but raised them for large-scale dealing. Whether to pursue cases of simple possession was left to the discretion of the police and prosecutors.

Pot became available through "house dealers" in Dutch youth clubs and coffee shops. Surprisingly, the use of pot by young people declined. The use rate is less than 10 percent of the U.S. rate. Professor Arnold Trebach has commented that the Dutch "have succeeded in making pot a boring subject to most of the youth of the country."

Jon Gettman is the national director of NORML (National Organization for Reform of the Marijuana Laws), which claims a membership of 5,000. He puts the argument for legalization this way:

> *When they consider marijuana's effect on the human body in the context of other commonly used drugs, such as alcohol, tobacco, sleeping pills and cold medications, people realize we have a double standard. Shouldn't adults make their own decisions about marijuana just as they do every day in the drug store?*

Gabriel G. Nahas, professor of pharmacology at the College of Physicians and Surgeons, is one of the leading opponents of decriminalizing marijuana. He points out that it is impossible to predict how much THC any "joint" may contain. The drug varies in strength from one plant to another. It even varies in cuttings taken from the same plant at different times of the day. Hence no package containing the drug could comply with the Food and Drug Administration requirement that its label state the exact amounts of chemicals it contains.

Nahas further notes that marijuana also contains benzopyrene, a cancer-causing substance that is 70 percent more abundant in pot smoke than in tobacco.

He concludes that "there is no pharmacological or medical justification for use of marijuana, the crude drug, in the treatment of specific ailments." Other experts strongly dispute Nahas's findings.

In 1986, when he was serving as U.S. attorney in New York, Rudolph Giuliani commented on the idea that legalization of marijuana would reduce crime. He pointed out that "marijuana has almost nothing to do with organized crime; if we decriminalized it tomorrow, the crime rate in Manhattan would remain virtually the same."

LEGALIZATION IN OTHER COUNTRIES

Both sides often cite Britain as an example of a country that has experimented with legalization. Its system started way back in 1926. Private doctors were authorized to prescribe maintenance doses for narcotics addicts. The addicts were registered, with their names recorded in government files.

Trial of the new system was eased by the fact that Britain had relatively few addicts. As late as the mid-1950s, the country still had only a few hundred. Street crime by addicts was virtually unknown.

The situation changed dramatically in the 1960s. This was a time of youthful turmoil and rebellion against the morals and manners of respectable society, in Britain as in the U.S. Drug abuse and the number of addicts rose steeply. For the first time, street crime became a serious problem.

The British government reacted sharply. Private doctors were forbidden to prescribe narcotics. Drug distribution to addicts became a strictly administered government program. Only a few specially licensed doctors could dispense narcotics.

The problem kept getting worse. Britain had 50,000 addicts by 1985. That was four times as many as were registered in 1980. Finally, in 1985 the program was jettisoned and legalization was repealed.

Decriminalization in various forms is also being tried in Switzerland and Holland. Heroin is technically illegal in Switzerland, but the city of Zurich allows open trafficking in the drug and injection of it in a park behind the central railroad station. A health center in the park distributes 6,000 clean needles a day in exchange for used ones, as a step toward combating the spread of AIDS.

Switzerland is thought likely to become the first European country to completely decriminalize the use and possession of small amounts of narcotics.

In Rotterdam, Holland, buying and selling heroin on the streets is illegal. But the police tolerate drug peddling inside dealers' apartments in one neighborhood. Dealers are arrested if they allow their customers to become a local nuisance or if they sell poor-quality, adulterated heroin.

Dutch authorities say that the number of addicts has declined in recent years. The addict population has also aged. Those in Rotterdam average about thirty years old. That is about ten years older than the average American addict. Dutch youth seem to have grown more aware of the dangers, and they tend to avoid drugs.

The authorities in both Switzerland and Holland have decided that harassment of users and small-time dealers serves no useful purpose. It only drives the prices up. But they admit that the addict populations of their countries are much more middle class and homogeneous than those of the U.S. Their systems might not work with so large and varied a population as America's.

In April 1989, an international congress of lawyers, doctors, politicians, academics, and police officers met in Rome, Italy, to discuss the drug problem. The delegates, drawn from a dozen Western countries, set up an International Anti-Prohibition League on Drugs. Acknowledging Europe's failure to find effective ways to cope with its escalating drug epidemic, they proposed the repeal of all laws banning drugs.

The congress issued a statement, declaring:

The crime that results [from keeping drugs illegal] endangers ordinary citizens and threatens the stability of states. The mod-

*ern version of prohibitionism has turned great cities into battle-
fields.*

"If drugs were legalized," said an Italian delegate, "the
Mafia would be hurt."

Two countries of Southeast Asia, Malaysia and
Singapore, have adopted harsh antidrug policies that are at
the opposite pole from legalization. Addicts are involuntarily
committed to lengthy terms in rehab centers without any
form of legal process. Rigorous semimilitary discipline is
maintained in these centers. In both countries, the death
penalty by hanging is imposed on those caught in possession of relatively small amounts of heroin, cocaine, or marijuana.

Results have been mixed. In Malaysia the addiction rate
has recently been rising. In Singapore the number of addicts
has dropped below its 1976 peak, but the problem remains
grave.

COMMUNITY ACTION

Growing numbers of Americans across the country have decided they cannot wait for the government's war against
drugs to end the scourge. Entire communities, as well as
groups of homeowners and apartment dwellers in neighborhoods taken over by dealers, have made up their minds to
organize and act together. Their actions have taken a fascinat-
ing variety of forms.

Some have adopted a dangerous tactic: direct confrontation with the dealers. Pioneers of this technique have been

the Beat Keepers of Los Angeles. They came together in groups and chased away the dealers operating around the famous intersection of Hollywood and Vine.

In Berkeley, California, the Francisco Street Community Group adopted a very different approach. After a fifteen-year-old boy was robbed at gunpoint by a crack dealer, fifteen members of the group filed suit in small-claims court against the owner of a crack house. Each plaintiff was eventually awarded $1,000. The landlord evicted his crack-dealing tenants.

The Berkeley group has since prepared a manual to teach others how to bring similar suits.

In Houston, Texas, a six-block slum area known as Link Valley was a center of drug dealing and violence. Residents of nearby areas formed the Stella Link Revitalization Coalition, a union of nine civic associations. They persuaded the police to mount massive sweeps of Link Valley. As soon as the dealers and their customers were gone, the coalition members moved in and laboriously cleaned up the neighborhood, house by house. Closely watched by the coalition and the police, the area has remained drug-free.

Community groups have found that the most valuable help they can offer the police is information. Neighborhood patrols often know the spots where dealing is underway better than the police do. Instead of confronting dealers—a tactic that can lead to violence—they record license numbers and descriptions of drug buyers and sellers. Phone calls to police hotlines can often bring mobile police detachments to the scene while the action is underway.

In Boston, community activists can call a police hotline that handles 300 to 500 calls a month. Police officials acknowledge that these tipsters provide information the police could not get any other way. One call in twelve results either in an arrest or in confiscation of drugs. The community people "know the dealers. They watch them up close."

The police warn against direct challenges to the heavily armed dealers. Citizens are advised to avoid physical confrontations and not to carry weapons. In several communities, leaders of antidrug crusades have been killed. One community uses the motto "Be vigilant, don't be a vigilante."

The people of Jackson County, Missouri, found a unique way to express their frustration over the government's failure to commit adequate resources to the war on drugs. An overwhelming 60 percent voted for a county sales tax to fund their own drug war.

In Kansas City, the Ad Hoc Group Against Crime harasses dealers by holding rallies near suspected drug houses. Sometimes the members drag a heavy wooden cross and an empty pine coffin past the houses. They sift through city records to track down the owners and pressure them to evict dealers and addicts. The group even offers rewards for callers to its twenty-four-hour hotline who supply tips that lead to arrests.

In New Orleans, the Third Shiloh Baptist Church bought two crack houses in order to shut them down. In Detroit, the Michigan Avenue Community Organization and Reach, Inc., buys abandoned houses, renovates them, and sells them to carefully picked tenants to prevent their falling into the hands of dealers.

In the economically depressed Cedar Grove area of Shreveport, Louisiana, nightly antidrug marches and rallies have been going on for months. The man who started and has often led them is Dick Gregory, comedian, civil-rights activist, and expert on dieting. Gregory told an interviewer:

I figure if you can get a foothold here, you can get one anywhere. This [drug situation] is so big, so complicated, it makes the civil-rights movement look like child's play.

Drug trafficking and violence in the formerly dealer-dominated and dangerous neighborhood have declined dramatically.

EDUCATION

"Just Say No!" has been a widely publicized antidrug slogan, aimed mostly at young people. But in view of the grim realities of the drug infestation in the nation's streets and playgrounds and even schools, the slogan has sometimes been scoffed at as merely a catchy phrase. The question on the mind of many has been, How do we turn the slogan into a genuine rule of behavior that youngsters will actually practice?

One answer, perhaps the indispensable answer, is antidrug education. It has two main goals. It seeks to give youngsters information that will prevent their starting on drugs. And it seeks to persuade those who have tried drugs to stop.

The most successful antidrug lessons have been found to be the ones that are the most realistic. They are based on the latest available scientific information. They are calm and factual, avoiding scare tactics rife with exaggerated and inaccurate statements. These only undermine the believability of educators.

Children who have tried marijuana, for instance, or who know others who use it, are unlikely to be impressed if teachers tell them that the drug will drive them crazy or kill them.

Even when teaching about hard drugs like heroin, cocaine, crack, or the "designer drugs," credible warnings are those limited to the true dangers.

School policies are an important teaching tool. Youngsters need to get the clear message that drug use will not be tolerated in or around the school. Even stronger lessons are learned when young people get the feeling that their entire community is united and active in the struggle against drugs.

Many schools bring police, representatives of local drug agencies, and reformed addicts into the classroom. Such visitors stimulate interest, heighten the school's credibility, and can impress some hard lessons on young minds.

Police commanders increasingly favor this use of their forces. They are frustrated by the overwhelming numbers of drug offenders and the seemingly infinite supply of drugs. Conventional police methods, many believe, have reached their limits. They are convinced that the real solution lies in preventing young people from getting involved with drugs in the first place.

Police Chief Charles A. Gruber of Shreveport, Louisiana, told a congressional committee: "For all our policing, we understand that law enforcement is not the solution to the problem of drugs in our society."

What police have been doing until now to fight drugs, said Earl Cronin of the Policemen's Association in Washington, D.C., is "like trying to drain the ocean with a teaspoon."

Specially trained police officers and sheriffs are going into elementary schools in many cities. They teach children how to be more assertive in refusing drugs, as well as ways of coping with stress.

One model program is called Drug Abuse Resistance

Education, or DARE. It was developed by the Los Angeles Police Department. It comprises seventeen lessons designed for third- and sixth-grade pupils. DARE has been adopted by two thousand localities in forty-nine states, three foreign countries, and Department of Defense schools overseas. It currently reaches 3 million schoolchildren.

Such programs, police experts contend, are more effective and are certainly cheaper than throwing youngsters into prison.

An occasional antidrug lesson occupying an otherwise unscheduled half hour cannot be expected to produce positive results. Successful programs start in kindergarten and continue on a regularly scheduled basis through high school.

In schools with sound antidrug programs, counseling is available in various forms. Students know they can seek out not only professional counselors on the staff but also teachers and administrators whom they know and trust.

An example of a highly successful program—one of many more or less similar ones that can be found throughout the entire country—is underway in the Levittown, New York, school district. It has set up its own Substance Abuse Task Force, consisting of students, parents, teachers, administrators, community leaders, and drug-abuse specialists. They work together toward the hopeful goal of making their town drug-free.

The task force sponsors Levittown Education Against Drugs Week (LEAD), which takes place in April. Every school in the district plans activities that include antidrug speakers, assemblies, and instructional programs. Activities include button-designing contests, writing songs and plays, movie presentations, discussion groups, and poster contests.

A recent study involved 22,500 sixth- and seventh-graders from forty-two schools in Kansas City, Missouri, and Kansas City, Kansas. Students at randomly selected schools were taught why they should avoid drugs and how to resist them. Homework assignments included role playing with family members, who were interviewed about family rules on drug use. Students in the remaining schools simply continued with their regularly scheduled programs.

A year later, students were asked if they had used drugs in the past month. The number who had done so was much lower in the schools that received the special training. A well-planned educational program had paid off.

In July 1990, the U.S. Department of Education issued a detailed drug-prevention curriculum to schools throughout the country. The schools can use it voluntarily or adapt it to fit into their ongoing programs. Entitled "Learning to Live Drug-Free," it covers kindergarten through the twelfth grade. The curriculum's goal is to help youngsters resist peer pressures and make healthy choices for their lives.

Drug prevention is still a developing skill. Even experts do not know with certainty what will work in any given situation. Constant evaluation is essential. Faculty, parents, and students can all provide useful feedback.

Advertising has become an increasingly used antidrug educational instrument. Volunteer groups such as the Partnership for a Drug-Free America have funded expensive nationwide campaigns. One full-page ad meant for employers was headlined "The last thing an addict needs from you is understanding." It urged employers to "get tough" with their employees and demand that any addicts among them either go into treatment or "get out."

Recent studies have shown that the most effective medium for reaching young people is radio rather than TV or print. They spend larger amounts of time listening than watching or reading.

One strong sixty-second radio ad pretended to be narrated by a teenage girl who had died of a cocaine overdose. "Hi, my name is Debbie," it began, "and I just got dressed for the last time." She had snorted cocaine the previous night, and couldn't sleep. "So I snuck into the medicine chest and took some cough medicine. That's all it took to kill me. . . ."

The drive to bring the drug epidemic under control is advancing on many fronts. The American people are aroused, and their government has declared total war.

Yet no honest portrayal of the overall picture can pretend that the war is being won. More drugs are getting through the nation's borders than ever before. Ever higher numbers of individuals are using and abusing them. Drug-related crime and violence are on the upswing, terrorizing and angering the population. Despite all the billions that have already been spent on the effort to bring it under control, the deadliest epidemic in America's history rages on unabated.

Perhaps it is time to stop all the rhetoric about the war on drugs. "War" implies an attainable goal of total victory. Such talk can only heighten the sense of frustration that bedevils the American people today.

A February 1990 *New York Times* editorial was titled "No More 'War on Drugs.'" It sounded a sensible note of realism:

> *Many social problems, however destructive, cannot be conquered—only managed and, with skill, reduced. That's true of drunken driving, teen-age pregnancy and venereal disease. And it is also true of drug abuse.*

Selected
Bibliography

BAKALAR, JAMES B., and LESTER GRINSPOON. *Drug Control in a Free Society.* Cambridge, England: Cambridge University Press, 1984. Advocates a liberal approach.

BAUM, JOANNE. *One Step over the Line: A No-Nonsense Guide to Recognizing and Treating Cocaine Dependency.* New York: Harper & Row, 1985. A therapist describes her work with addicts. Numerous case studies.

BESCHNER, GEORGE, and ALFRED S. FRIEDMAN, eds. *Teen Drug Use.* Lexington, MA: D. C. Heath, 1986. A collection of essays by noted experts.

BRECHER, EDWARD. *Licit and Illicit Drugs.* Boston: Little, Brown, 1972. A classic compilation of facts and a primer on addiction.

DALEY, DENNIS C., and JUDY MILLER. *A Parents' Guide to Alcoholism and Drug Abuse.* Newport, RI: Edgehill, 1989. Useful handbook.

GUGLIOTTA, GUY, and JEFF LEEN. *Kings of Cocaine: An Astonishing True Story of Murder, Money, and Corruption.* New York: Simon & Schuster, 1989. Excitingly told investigation by two journalists.

INCIARDI, JAMES A. *The War on Drugs: Heroin, Cocaine, Crime, and Public Policy.* Mountain View, CA: Mayfield, 1984. Challenges some widely accepted views.

KIRSCH, M. M. *Designer Drugs: Crack, Dust, Ecstasy, MPTP, Crystal, China White.* Minneapolis, MN: Comp Parc Publications, 1986. Extensive interviews with researchers, physicians, police, underground chemists, dealers, and users.

LISKA, KEN. *The Pharmacist's Guide to the Most Misused and Abused Drugs in America.* New York: Collier Books/Macmillan, 1988. Complete guide to commonly abused drugs.

MORRISON, MARTHA. *White Rabbit: A Woman Doctor's Story of Her Addiction and Recovery.* New York: Crown, 1988. Story of a multiple drug abuser.

SHANNON, ELAINE. *Desperadoes: Latin Drug Lords, U. S. Lawmen, and the War America Can't Win.* New York: Viking, 1988. Colorfully told story, with emphasis on kidnap-murder of U.S. agent "Kiki" Camarena. Basis of NBC-TV miniseries.

STORTI, ED, and JANET KELLER. *Crisis Intervention: Acting against Addiction.* New York: Crown, 1988. A technique for getting addicts into treatment.

TREBACH, ARNOLD S. *The Great Drug War: Radical Proposals That Could Make America Safe Again.* New York: Macmillan, 1987. Attacks many conventional notions, offers innovative ideas.

WEISS, ROGER D., and STEVEN M. MIRIN. *Cocaine.* Washington, D.C.: American Psychiatric Press, 1987. Brief, helpful study by two psychiatrists.

SUGGESTIONS FOR YOUNG READERS

AUGUST, PAUL N. *Drugs and Women.* New York: Chelsea House, 1987 (*Encyclopedia of Psychoactive Drugs* series). Investigates special problems of drug-involved women.

BACH, JULIE S., ed. *Drug Abuse: Opposing Viewpoints.* St. Paul, MN: Greenhaven Press, 1988. Pro and con arguments.

BERGER, GILDA. *Crack: The New Drug Epidemic.* New York: Franklin Watts, 1987. The drug's social, psychological, and medical effects.

————. *Drug Abuse: The Impact on Society.* New York: Franklin Watts, 1988. A broad-ranging study.

————. *Drug Testing.* New York: Franklin Watts, 1986. The many-sided controversy.

COHEN, SUSAN, and DANIEL COHEN. *What You Can Believe about Drugs: An Honest and Unhysterical Guide for Teens.* New York: Holt, 1988. Straightforward and tolerant; challenges alarmist cliches.

DEBNER-BIALKE, CLAUDIA, ed. *Chemical Dependency: Opposing Viewpoints.* St. Paul, MN: Greenhaven Press, 1985. Pro and con arguments. One of a series.

HARRIS, JONATHAN. *Drugged Athletes: The Crisis in American Sports.* New York: Four Winds Press, 1987. Why athletes use drugs; modes of treatment and prevention.

HOOBLER, THOMAS, and DOROTHY HOOBLER. *Drugs and Crime.* New York: Chelsea House, 1988 (*Encyclopedia of Psychoactive Drugs* series). Examines the complex cause-and-effect relationship.

JUSSIM, DANIEL. *Drug Tests and Polygraphs.* New York: Messner, 1987. First half gives brief discussion of testing.

MARSHALL, ELLIOTT. *Legalization: A Debate.* New York: Chelsea House, 1988 (*Encyclopedia of Psychoactive Drugs* series). Pro and con arguments.

RODGERS, JOANN E. *Drugs and Sexual Behavior.* New York: Chelsea House, 1988 (*Encyclopedia of Psychoactive Drugs* series). The effects of drugs on relations between the sexes.

Index